ALSO BY TOM PETERS

*In Search of Excellence*
(with Robert H. Waterman, Jr.)

*A Passion for Excellence*
(with Nancy Austin)

*Thriving on Chaos*

*Liberation Management*

*The Tom Peters Seminar*

*The Pursuit of WOW!*

*The Circle of Innovation*

Reinventing Work:
*the Project50*
*the Brand You50*

# Tom

# Peters

## REINVENTING WORK:

ALFRED A. KNOPF, INC.

NEW YORK 1999

# *the*
# professional
# service firm
# 50

**Or:** FIFTY WAYS TO TRANSFORM YOUR "DEPARTMENT"
INTO A *PROFESSIONAL SERVICE FIRM*
WHOSE TRADEMARKS ARE PASSION AND INNOVATION!

www.randomhouse.com

Knopf, Borzoi Books, and the colophon are registered trademarks
of Random House, Inc.

Grateful acknowledgment is made to the following for permission
to reprint previously published material:
*The Free Press:* Excerpts from *True Professionalism: The Courage to
Care About Your People, Your Clients, and Your Career* by David H.
Maister. Copyright © 1997 by David H. Maister. Reprinted with the
permission of The Free Press, a division of Simon & Schuster, Inc.
*Prentice-Hall, Inc.:* Excerpts from *Corporate Strategy and the Search
for Ethics* by R. Edward Freeman and Daniel R. Gilbert. Copyright
© 1988 by R. Edward Freeman and Daniel R. Gilbert. Reprinted by
permission of Prentice-Hall, Inc., Upper Saddle River, N.J.

Library of Congress Cataloging-in-Publication Data
Peters, Thomas J.
    The professional service firm50: transform your "depart-
ment" into a professional service firm whose trademarks are
passion and innovation! / by Tom Peters.— 1st ed.
        p.   cm.—(Reinventing work)
    ISBN 0-375-40771-5
    1. Service industries—Management.  2. Customer
services—Management.  I. Title.  II. Series.
HD9980.5.P398   1999
658.8'12—dc21
                                                        99-33616
                                                            CIP

Manufactured in the United States of America
First Edition

# DEDICATIONS

Marvin Bower, grand panjandrum of McKinsey & Co. (Mr. PSF!)

David Ogilvy, 1911–1999, guru and founder of Ogilvy & Mather

David Kelley, IDEO Design & Product Development, the only company (other than my own) I'd ever consider working for

# 5oLISTS: CREDO

CUBICLE SLAVES ... HACK OFF YOUR TIES ... FLIP OFF YOUR HEELS ...

THE WORK CAN BE COOL!

THE WORK CAN BE BEAUTIFUL!

THE WORK CAN BE FUN!

THE WORK CAN MAKE A DIFFERENCE!

Y-O-U CAN MAKE A DIFFERENCE!

BASH YOUR CUBICLE WALLS!

RIP UP YOUR DILBERT CARTOONS!

THE WHITE COLLAR REVOLUTION IS ON!

90 PERCENT OF OUR JOBS ARE IN JEOPARDY!

TAKE CHARGE OF YOUR LIFE!

SUBVERT THE HIERARCHY!

MAKE EVERY PROJECT A WOW!

BE DISTINCT ... OR EXTINCT!

*IT'S A NEW MILLENNIUM: IF NOT NOW ... W-H-E-N?*

# 5oLISTS:
# SERIES INTRODUCTION

**We aren't knocking Dilbert. Who would dare? But we do believe that work can be cool. THAT THE WORK MATTERS.**
—Tom Peters

*Work—yours and mine—as we know it today will be reinvented in the next ten years. It's as simple as that. And as profound. Here's why ...*

*The tough old union militant remembers. In 1970 (not exactly an eon ago) it took 108 guys some five days to unload a ship full of timber. And now? Container daze: eight guys ... one day.*

*It happened on the farm when the thresher came along. It happened in the distribution center when the forklift arrived. And it happened dockside.*

*But, hey, it's the new millennium. Ninety-plus percent of us—even in so-called "manufacturing" companies— work at white collar jobs. Fact: We haven't touched—or really even bothered with—white collar productivity. Never. Until now ...*

*It's a brand-new ballgame. THE WHITE COLLAR REVOLUTION IS ON! The accounting "shop" is coming under the same productivity searchlight that those docks did. And we think we have an inkling of what the new rules will be.*

*The revolution: Information systems. Information technology. Enterprise Resource Planning systems. Intranets.*

*Knowledge-capital-management schemes. Enterprise Customer Management. The Web. Globalization. Global deregulation. Etc. Etc. All fueling a—no hype—once every 100, 200, 500(?) years revolution.*

*Which brings us to this new series of books—which aims at nothing less than a total reinvention of work (how we think about it, undertake it, bring ourselves to it). The work-reinvention revolution turns out to be a matchless opportunity for liberation—in our organizations and in our lives.*

*This book is part of the first release in a series of what we call 50Lists. Each book describes a different aspect of work in the New Economy. Each book is built on 50 essential ideas.*               —The Editors

# CONTENTS

## IV. Live with 'Em!

## VII. Talent!

## VIII. It's Ours!

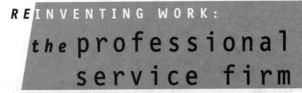

REINVENTING WORK:
*the* professional
service firm

50

# INTRODUCTION:
# THE INEXORABLE
# "PSF" LOGIC

The White Collar Revolution will envelop 90+ percent of us. And quickly. The commonplace, if traumatic, changes that came to the factory, the distribution center, and the London docks are now racing toward the relatively unscathed world of "purchasing," "finance," "HR," "IT," etc.

Of course, we had "re-engineering" and "downsizing" in the nineties. But truth is, work-in-finance today looks about the way it did decades ago. We pass "papers"—electronically, to be sure—but the topics are about the same. And the processing delays are maddening as ever. As are the petty tyrants who oversee the processes. (Witness Dilbert's monumental popularity; the comic strip depicts my dad's day in the Credit and Collections Dept. at the Baltimore Gas & Electric Company, circa 1955, as accurately as it captures white collar world at the millennium's turn.)

But—I repeat—all that is about to change. So-called Enterprise Resource Planning systems from SAP, PeopleSoft, Baan, et al. will hit high gear within the next decade. Clumsy knowledge management and knowledge-sharing systems will gather a full head of steam . . . or, should I say, a light-speed flow of bits.

Those of us in jeopardy—90+ percent, don't forget!—must invent a new game. A *hot* game that transforms "accounting" from the butt of a million jokes about "use-less overhead," "purposeful obfuscators," and "petty bureaucrats" to the … ta da … **scintillating center of value added through knowledge capital accumulation.**

Sound too grand for you? Fine.

But … then …

# what's the (your) alternative?

## AN ANSWER/T-H-E ANSWER?

I contend there *is* an alternative, *an* answer even. And that is—and long has been—right under our collective noses. To wit: the "real" Professional Service Firm, or PSF. À la McKinsey & Co., Chiat/Day, Arthur Andersen. And Andersen Consulting. IDEO. And EDS. Pricewaterhouse-Coopers. Kleiner Perkins Caufield & Byers. Wilson, Sonsini, Goodrich & Rosati. Etc.

These firms can be tiny … or huge. (EDS employs well over 100,000 people.) But regardless of size, they per-form pure intellectually based services, own damn little in the way of hard assets, and sometimes deposit billions of $$$$ on the bottom line. They do Good Work. Valuable Work. And, often, Important Work.

**Moreover, Life in a PSF is about as far a cry from DilbertDrones in DrearyVille (a.k.a. "Departments") as one can imagine.**

| PSF-WORLD | A DAY IN THE FINANCE DEPT./ETC. |
| --- | --- |
| Out of the office. (At the client's.) | In the office. |
| Lunch with a cool dude/ dudette, tapping her-his brain. | Lunch with the same old folks. |
| At work on a WOW! Project! | Ticking off an imposing but uninspiring "to-do" list. |
| Getting ready for a crucial review with a senior client exec, two days from now. (Super Bowl time!) | Working with close colleagues on the nuances re: latest memo "up-the-chain." |
| Going over the design of the client presentation with the graphic arts specialist. | Huh? |
| Working with outsiders on a cool market analysis. | Hangin' with the same old folks! |
| Two brainstorming meetings —most attendees are not from our dept. (Half are outsiders/strangers.) | Six hopelessly bureaucratic meetings with the same old turf-guarding bureaucrats! |
| Phone call with my boss to (1) review current project status (she wants a lot more WOW!!) and (2) scope next client project. | Called in by boss to review carefully crafted, passionless memo heading "up the chain." |
| Phone call: You're being re-cruited for a cool new project by a highly regarded senior professional in "The Firm." | Bitching about "politics-as-usual" at the water cooler. |

| PSF-WORLD | A DAY IN THE FINANCE DEPT./ETC. |
|---|---|
| In-depth interviews with two client experts. | Same old sources. |
| Cocktails (or racquetball!) with a phat pal you'd like to recruit someday. | After-work beers with same-old-buddies ... to complain about the same-old-shit. |
| Mentally and emotionally drained at the end of the day. | Bored outta my mind. (Again.) |
| Vibrating with excitement. | Need those beers! |

So why have we left these firms out in the cold for so long? Why haven't we studied them? **(We haven't. Period.)** I think there is an answer. In short: We didn't take them seriously! When I joined McKinsey & Co. in 1974, the consultants ... and lawyers ... and accountants and ad agency denizens were considered the bloodsuckers, the parasites living off the sweat of real men's—USW, UMW, and UAW members'—brows.

And then a funny thing happened.

# We woke up one morning and discovered ...
# we'd won!

The economy had taken a 180-degree turn. Bill Gates was the richest man in the world ... and the "soft guys," the "service guys," ruled. From Hollywood to Silicon Valley ... to a revived (branding *über Alles!*) Madison Avenue.

And so we started jawing about "virtual organizations" and "knowledge capital accumulation." Exotic, new stuff. And we imagined that we had to invent a brand-new wheel.

# Not so!

I'll be the first to acknowledge that there are crappy professional service firms … just as there are incompetent retailers and second basemen who bat .200. But the pick of the litter—just as with retailing—have a lot to teach us. Teach us about, say, scintillating projects that add value. I.e.: Work that Matters!

## THE "MODEL"

Our model is simple. And it will be expanded upon in this book and others in this *50List* series. To wit:

### New Work: Core Model

Point-of-impact for this millennial meteor: the white collar worker (**a.k.a.: you, me!**).

Those who survive—on or off a corporate payroll—will jettison (almost) everything they've learned and **(1)** adopt the attributes/attitudes of a PSF/Professional Service Firm. (The subject of this book.) They will behave as **(2)** de facto (if not yet de jure) independent contractors, or what I call Brand Yous. (Please see *the Brand You50.*) I.e., survivors will "be" a product … and exhibit clear-cut distinction at … s-o-m-e-t-h-i-n-g. And (3) the bottom line or base element for the PSF, Brand You, and the White Collar Revolution: the Project. (Please see *the Project50.*)

## EXCITING "BOTTOM LINE"

So that's the crux of the story!

# Liberation!

# Transforming work!

# Performing Work that Matters!

# Becoming Brand You!

# Living in a scintillating Professional Service Firm … a Department that Matters!

We think that this logical case for transforming work is airtight. So join us on this …

# Adventure Toward Work that
# WOWs!

What follows is a portrait. A portrait of a "Department" transforming itself into a full-fledged Professional Service Firm. The aspirations are grand. The challenges are enormous.

Even if the logic rings true and the heart is willing, can you expect to pull off "all this stuff" (among other things, some 200 "To Do's")?

# No!

What you *can* do:

* Treat this as the portrait it is. **Imagine a Different World for your "Dept."** Talk with colleagues about the portrait that does emerge ... and your collective aspirations. (We urge you to dream!) DOES THIS MAKE SENSE? THE BASIC ARGUMENT? THE PARTICULARS?

* Go through the Main List of 50+ items and select, using some ranking scheme, **10** that make the most sense for you and your colleagues. (That are most *important* ... and that are *surprising/provocative*.) Discuss the 10.

* Select a couple of action steps (To Do's) from each of the 10 selected items. Find a Volunteer Champion, and consider an action plan for going after each one.

* Alternatively, assign priorities to each of the seven sections in the book. Choose a Discussion Leader for each section. Once every two weeks, say, schedule a session to review a selected section; perhaps invite a relevant outsider to talk about the content. Consider practical Next Steps at the end of each discussion session.

There are 100 other ways to skin this cat. My point: We don't expect you to bite off the entire challenge in one crunchy chomp. We do hope you'll consider some scheme —of your choosing—for walking through the content in a measured way.

## WHO IS THIS BOOK FOR?

*The* idea of "PSF 50": Turning a "Dept." into a full-fledged, WOW-Project-obsessed **P**rofessional **S**ervice **F**irm.

So … does that mean this is a book for bosses? Yes. And no.

**Yes:** The key idea is that the HR Dept. head is now … Managing Partner, HR Inc. **No:** We will *all*—survivors!—inhabit PSFs. We *all* must learn the ways of these exceptional institutions, and thence create mini-PSFs in every setting we inhabit. The PSF "mindset" is as appropriate/important to the neophyte 23-year-old professional as it is to that Department Head, age 43.

# I. PSF = inc.
# + clients
# + projects!

*the*

# professional
# service firm
# 50

>>>>>>>>

# 1.

It all starts in your head. Imagine:

## You are no longer "HR Director."

## You are Managing Partner/Managing Director of HR Inc.... a wholly owned subsidiary of the "ABC Division" of the "XYZ Corp."

The starting point of all significant change is mindset. I.e.: shifting from the internally focused, "task" mindset to a fanatical "Incredible-Client-Service-through-Awesome-Projects" mindset. Per this model, your group is a no-baloney, knock-their-socks-off independent entity ... which just happens to be currently associated with that parent "corporation."

### *The Nub*

## Today is a very cool day!

It is *not* another ho-hum day in HR ... Purchasing ... Finance ... whatever. This is opening night at that restaurant you've always dreamed of starting or the play you've been working on for ten months.

That is: The *new* doors are open … at HR Inc. or Purchasing Inc. or Finance Inc. There are flowers—voluptuous alstroemeria in February—on the reception desk. There is a bright red ribbon to be cut as you get off the ninth-floor elevator.

In short: A new Professional Service Firm is born!

# Hooray!

You (and your colleagues) are your own boss (bosses). The new calling cards read, de facto, if not de jure, Purchasing Inc., a subsidiary of the "ABC Division" of the "XYZ Corp."

Oh, yes, did I forget to mention: **You're scared shitless.** Just like I was in 1981, the day after I officially—and unceremoniously—finished my seven-year hitch at McKinsey & Co. In one quick breath I went from being a partner at a prestigious consulting company (most prestigious professional service firm in the world?!) to one guy working out of the spare bedroom in his apartment at 355 Fulton Street, Palo Alto, California.

It's cool. Very cool. And it's scary. As Hell. But wouldn't you rather be scared than racing toward extinction? Because in today's White Collar Revolution only the cool/paranoid/WOW!makers will survive. **(No kidding.)**

**Cool:** As PSFers, I/you/we can get on with the challenge of building a great "practice" (McKinsey & Co., lawyers and accountants all call their "work" a *practice*) based on the *things-we-really-care-about … and mean to* *stand for.* **Scary:** Got to cover the payroll ... and pay the rent and phone bill ... starting now. (Not to mention groceries.)

This exquisite tension, incidentally, will mark the rest of your Professional Service Firm career: the joy of limitless potential ... *and* the terror of bringing home—or not—the bacon.

**"Think Inc."** That's what I call this first of 50 PSF Commandments. And, first for a reason. I.e.: It's a big deal. (Why else the No. 1 designation?) It's 10 percent tangible. (How about new calling cards, even if you aren't an official subsidiary?) And 90 percent intangible: It's the "PSF Attitude."

The

# Professional Service Firm Attitude!

Yes ... a-t-t-i-t-u-d-e! Dictionary definition: "A state of mind or feeling with regard to some matter." How's this for an attitude: The band of Sisters and Brothers at Purchasing Inc. is about to embark on an Adventure, a Journey to Greatness. (Hey ... why the Hell not? *All* of our jobs—today—are in grave jeopardy.) Your aim: Knock Your Clients' Socks Off with Really Cool Work. Each project will be a no-baloney WOW! Project.

Can you do all this—and save your collective butts—by tomorrow morning? **No!** But can you start talking about the PSF Attitude ... *right now?* Yes! Yes! A hundred times over: **Yes!** (As in: What are *you*—you *all*—waiting for? Hint: The world is definitely not waiting for you.)

**1.** What if ...? What if we signed a Secret Pact ... and declared ourselves a full-fledged Professional Service Firm right now? What—*exactly*—would we do differently?

# List 10–25 items.

**2.** In the next 10 days, round up your colleagues and visit two "real" professional service firms you admire. (One small, one somewhat larger.) Hold an open-ended discussion: Who are they? What are they? How—**10 or more ways!**—are they different from our "Department"?

**3.** This ain't gonna be final ... but draft a Manifesto. (**"WE AT PURCHASING INC. BELIEVE ..."** or some such.) Put your heart and soul and passion and dreams into it. Pass it around. Discuss it. Edit it. Refine it. Use it to help you clarify where you are today, where you want to be ... and how you're going to strive to get there.

# 1a.

## COMMIT "COOL."

### The Nub

Words matter. (A lot.) (What do you expect me to say? I do words for a living!) "Cool"—or Kewl or phat or **fly-phat**—are words we don't ordinarily associate with accounting "departments" or HR "departments."

# Why not?

*My answer to "why not":*
(1) habit … (2) imagination (the lack thereof). The un-abashed goal of this book: Change all that! Make it—our joint—phat!

*In short:*
I want **"Cool Accounting Dept."** to be as common as dirt!

*My reasoning:*
First, accounting **is** cool. It **is** important. It **can** have impact. It **can** be exciting. It **can** be beautiful. (I *love* a simple, clear P&L or other financial report as much as I *love* a good symphony. Well … almost as much.) Second, I love *my* work … and I think it's cool … and I've spent my life in professional services.

I (desperately) want you to feel the way I do. (And I'm frustrated if you don't.)

# What we do … m-a-t-t-e-r-s.

Let's make it c-o-o-l … or die trying!

Okay?

T.T.D./Cool!

**1.** Write down—alone, or with two or three pals—10 succinct statements that describe a "Cool" Acctg., Purch., IS, or HR department. (Spend serious time on this.)

**2.** Shop your "Cool Acctg. Dept." description around with Clients. Get their input. Edit.

**3.** Publish (at least among your colleagues) a "Cool" Manifesto.

## 4. Talk up Cool.

**5.** Please take Nos. 1–4 above … **very** … seriously. (It's nothing less than your life we're talking about! Seriously redux.)

# 2.

## Client service is *the* name of *the* game.

And that's a-l-l, folks. The reality: You exist to *serve* clients. They *pay* your bills. If you don't perform, they can —and will—take their custom elsewhere. "Real" PSFs— Andersen, EDS, etc.—obsess about Clients. There's no other way to put it. (Alas, one rarely even hears the word "client" during a visit to an average HR or Purchasing Dept.)

### The Nub

Remember that lemonade stand you had as a kid? Remember the thrill of the first "customer" actually forking over a dime for a cup of your stuff? That "customer" is now your "Client." The transaction is no doubt a good deal more sophisticated, but the basic truth remains the same: If you want that customer-Client to come back for more, your lemonade better be damn good/a.k.a. WOW! So, too, your attitude.

Clients are cool. **Clients are a rush.** And yet in "Dept." world the Client often gets lost in the shuffle. Or, worse yet, is seen as a nuisance. Or doesn't even really seem to exist at all.

Look, I've had rotten Clients. Clients who demeaned me or made completely unreasonable demands. (And a few who didn't pay their bills.) But I also know where my bread is buttered. I clearly remember the-very-first-check-I-received after I left McKinsey & Co. and set up shop on my own. (It was from American Express. *Thank you, Amex.*) Along with money, the check brought me an exhilarating feeling of freedom and power and a job well done. Celebration Time!

That was the day...

# I fell wildly in love with ...Clients.

I love to goad my Clients. Push them to tackle new challenges, to soar to unimagined heights. I am a born (or made) agitator. But I do it (I pray) with respect and always with their interests in mind. I want them to see stellar (amazing/supercalifragilisticexpialidocious) results *and*, not so incidentally, I want to be well paid for my efforts. The Client is my matchless Validity Certification Device!

Am I special? **No.** Not in PSF World. "We" (PSFers) may moan about Clients. Bitterly. But they are—in the end— the reason we exist. I may think my seminars are exciting, and sexy as Hell; but if nobody shows up ... I'm talking to myself. I've got a problem. Major.

Clients? I love 'em. The more hard-assed the better!

**(Axiom:** We are *exactly* as good as the Clients who push us the hardest.)

## "CLIENT" VS. "CUSTOMER"

What's in a word? A lot! Take "customer." And "client." McKinsey & Co. calls the people who pay the bills … clients. Make that **C**lients. Safeway, on the other hand, has customers.

And … never (more or less) … the twain shall meet.

# A "Client" is …

* a *partner*

* someone with whom I have an *intimate relationship*

* in it with me for the *long haul*

* someone with whom I *co-invent* the future

* a person/organization in whose outcomes I have a big *personal stake*

* someone with whom I have an *emotional bond*

* someone with whom I can't work if *trust* is not paramount

* a *fellow professional* who, like me, wrestles with intractable problems

* the source of my *reputation* (for better or for worse)

* my No. 1 *"word-of-mouth"* marketer!

* someone who *grows* with me

* someone who *loses when I lose*

* someone who *wins when I win*

  Okay? (I.e.: Right?) (Or not?)

1. Start now. Use the word ... **C**-l-i-e-n-t.

## Period. And forevermore.

Words matter.

The **C**lient = Your life. (In PSF-land.)

The **C**lient pays the bills. (Or ... doesn't.)

The **C**lient says you're reliable, trustworthy. (Or ... not.)

The **C**lient says you're phat. (Or ... not.)

2. Okay, let's start at square one: Who *are* your **C**lients? Begin with a list. Easier said than done. You "serve" all sorts of people and groups. Who are the lead players? The supporting cast? Spend a lot of time on this seemingly simple task.

3. What do you *really know* about your Clients? **Professionally? Personally?** Start a file (with a file/account number) for each Client. Start filling it up. Any and all information goes in there ... including quirks and eccentricities, which are often the clue to delivering superb results. Get everyone in the Dept./PSF to contribute. Hint: Develop formal Client Files with Client file numbers even if you have no intention of declaring your unit a full-fledged PSF.

4. Concoct a press release for your Clients. And a press kit! Put yourself officially in business as a Client-Serving PSF—again even if you officially remain a "Dept." State your aims and purpose as a Client-Serving PSF ... clearly. (More later on this point.)

# 3.

## SELECT CLIENTS VERY CAREFULLY.

It's axiomatic:

**You're as good—or as bad—as the character of your Client List.**

**In a very real sense, you *are* your Client List!**

### The Nub

It really is that simple:

## YOU *ARE* YOUR CLIENTS!

If I run a home-furnishings company (I am involved in one, in a kibitzing kind of way) and somebody asks me what we do … it takes all of 10 seconds before I somehow work in the fact that Neiman Marcus is one of our customers. (Clients … damn it! I insist that we use "the word" in our home-furnishings company.)

**I (we!/PSFers) am/are defined by the people we "sell to" … as much as by the particulars of the product or service we sell.**

Lesson/Axiom: Choose damn carefully! Because you are also as much who your Clients are *not* as who they are.

Since 75 percent of the audience at my seminars work in "Depts.," I can already hear you flipping to the next point ... or tossing the book down: "Doesn't apply. We're in-house, and we gotta serve everybody we're told to."

"Yes." And "no." Mainly ... **NO.**

You do "gotta" answer the phone. True enough. But not all internal Clients are created equal. As a Senior Training Officer in the HR Dept., you are serving, say, nine retail stores. Dick, Bob, and David are store managers of the old school: They think your new ideas are silly ... if not outrageous. Sam, Jane, Mike, and Anna sit on the fence. (The world abounds in fence-sitters. Live with it.) But Arlene just got appointed store manager, at the young age of 27. She is a go-getter ... curious, cool, courageous ... and imaginative as Hell. You took her to lunch last week, and she is "totally excited" (her words) about the new, unconventional customer service course that you desperately want to pilot ... soon ... somewhere. Likewise, Harold, though older, sees a new world descending on retail; he, too, is keen to push his staff to new and different heights.

Great! Arlene and Harold are your "Neiman Marcuses." That is, you won't ignore the other seven store managers. You can't. You shouldn't. But you *will* shower Arlene and Harold with attention ... enlist them as co-conspirators in your effort to "Reinvent Customer Service" ... or some such. Okay?

I.e.: You will be known by the quality of your internal customers as much as a home-furnishings company will be known by the quality of its external customers ... um, **C**lients.

## T.T.D./Client Selection Rules!

**1.** Your formal Client files are in place. (See No. 2 above.) So now let's start sorting: Who is "cool"? Who are the standpatters?

Approach each "cool" prospect.(Prospects! That's what they are, relative to your Cool Plans. Right?) Start the discussion about their "signing up" as co-inventors/ co-conspirators in your revolution.(You are making a revolution ... eh?) Your job here: Inspire them with your passion.

**2.** Keep a detailed log: With what Clients am I investing my most precious resource ... T-I-M-E? Are my Clients people I take a real shine to? If not, what specifically can I do about it? E.g., look for new and interesting contacts in the Client organization and propose new projects to test their reaction to revolutionary ventures.

**3.** Explicitly concentrate your efforts on a (very?) few Cool Clients. E.g.: Schedule regular meetings to share bold ideas with those Clients. Meticulously chart joint progress.(Keep stretching. Together.)

# 3a.

## The Nub

Tom Peters is perceived as "cool" **if** his Clients are Cool. Tom Peters is not only cool but "hot" **if** his Clients are Hot and constantly pushing him to new heights.

I simply don't want Clients who are going to be satisfied with "acceptable work." I want Clients who **demand** that I deliver and push. Hey, I'm as prone to the occasional halfhearted effort as the next guy/gal. That's why I…**bless**…those Clients who hold my feet/heart/mind to the fire. I want Clients who make me dig deep, who push/drag/shove me out of my box (we all have one) and force me to use every ounce of my talents. Sure, I may curse them while it's happening, but I bless them once it's over. Because I come out the other end a better/stronger/smarter person.

## Message (big): Seek out cool Clients who (1) define you and (2) help you grow.

(Big) addendum to message: "Cool" Clients are not necessarily—or even often—the "biggest" clients. Bulk is not the goal! Cool is!

**1.** Invest — heavily!—in terribly "cool" Clients who will test you. And help you grow … personally … and professionally.(Redux: Dis-invest in those who don't.)

**2. The best possible Client is an on-the-make youngster-revolutionary, probably operating at the edge of or entirely off the organizational radar screen, who will become your Ardent Partner in Revolution. Find her/him/ them.**

(These are the people I've sought out for years. They have made me!)

# 3b.

## F-I-R-E CLIENTS … UPON OCCASION.

(And perhaps not that rarely.) The greatest adman of them all, the late David Ogilvy, bragged of having fired many more Clients than had fired him.

Why? Some Clients turn out to be jerks. Some initially terrific Clients eventually wear you and your staff out. Of course, some dreary Clients can be brought to life … and when you're able to infuse Clients with your excitement and convince them to take risks they hadn't even considered, well, that's one of the most exciting moments of all. Nonetheless … you must prune your Client List from time to time.

*Remember:* Your Client List is what you stand for/what you are!

### The Nub

"Dull clients make for a dull Jane/Jack." It's that simple. Well, it's not that simple. At all. The "big" client—internal or external—brings in the big bucks. (I can do my sums!) Yet at some point you have perhaps gotten too close. You aren't an Agent Provocateur anymore. You're family. Family = Good. (Comfy. Dependable revenue stream.) Family = Potentially bad. (We lose our edge. Complacency sets in. Can mediocrity be far behind?)

In short, I have walked away from lucrative clients, because we were … at that moment … boring each other to death. I knew "too much." (And, I quickly add, vice versa.) I need to know a lot about a Client's business to be helpful with practical, implementation issues. But then—at some subtle point—I may cross over from knowing "enough to be helpful" to "too much to be provocative." And/or I get hooked on the revenue stream and am no longer pushing or willing to push the Client to the point of irritation. Big whoops. Why?

## Good PSFs live to irritate!

To push and prod … beyond the comfort zone. Again and again. And yet again.

## THE MAISTER TEST

The following is extracted from PSF guru David Maister's *True Professionalism*:

> Professional success requires more than talent. Among other things, it requires drive, initiative, commitment, involvement, and—above all—enthusiasm. Yet these things are often missing from professionals' lives....
>
> Think back on all the work you have done in the past year or so, and divide it among three categories, the first of which is "God, I love this! This is why I do what I do!" The second category is "It's OK, I can tolerate it—it's what I do for a living." The third category is "I hate this part—I wish I could get rid of this junk!"
>
> Let me report the results of putting this question to top professionals in prestige firms around the world. The typical answers I am given are 20 percent to 25 percent for "God, I love this!"; 60 percent to 70 percent for "I can tolerate it"; and 5 percent to 20 percent for "I hate this part." In other words, the typical professional in a top firm is positively enjoying his or her work about one day a week.
>
> Now, a second question: Think about all of the clients you have served in the past year and, again, divide them into three categories. Category one is "I like these people, and their industry interests me." (Yes, I know I'm combining two things.) Category two is "I can tolerate these people and their business is OK—neither fascinating nor boring."

*Category three is "I'm professional enough that I would never say this to them, and I'll still do my best for them, but the truth is that these are not my kind of people, and I have no interest in their industry."...*

*Typical answers from top professionals around the world are 30 percent to 35 percent for "I like these people"; 50 percent to 60 percent "I can tolerate these people"; and 5 percent to 20 percent for "These are not my kind of people."...*

*These estimates provide the single biggest reason to introduce some energy into your professional life. Why spend the majority of that life working on tolerable stuff for acceptable clients when, with some effort in (for example) client relations, marketing, and selling, you can spend your days working on exciting things for interesting people?*

TOM COMMENT: **Amen!**

## T.T.D./Dump Dud Clients!

1. Examine your client list v-e-r-y carefully.

### What's fresh? What's stale?

Consider "firing"—or laying off for a while—the stale sorts.

2. When you wake up in the morning, are there Clients you dread seeing? If so, consider—seriously!—dumping them. Again: at least for a while.

**3.** **Rank each Client** on a scale of 1 to 10: 1 = Dull as dishwater. 10 = Provokes me and stretches me continually. Look closely at all of those who score 1–4. Do the ranking again: 1 = Really dreary. 10 = Love to be around 'em. Again, look closely at the 1–4 set. (This *is* your life. You *are* your Clients. It is fair, sensible, and imperative to make these judgments. To dodge doing so shows a lack of integrity.)

# 4.

## TURN EVERY "TASK" INTO A PROJECT.

## PSF = Client. PSF = Project.

**100 percent** of your time should be occupied by discrete projects. This is not pie-in-the-sky. The most mundane tasks—in the hands of a thoughtful PSFer—can be converted into interesting probes into the heart of a business system; that is, Projects Worth Doing. (E.g.: A McKinsey & Co. colleague, Bill Matassoni, converted a "dreary" library reorg chore into a strategic knowledge-sharing initiative that changed the entire company.)

### *The Nub*

## A terrific "PSF" is ... (1) COOL People ... (2) doing COOL Projects ... (3) with COOL Clients.

And that's all, folks!

One hundred percent of my professional time and, truth be known, most of my personal time is occupied (preoccupied) by ... P-R-O-J-E-C-T-S. This book. A column of 1,500 words for *Forbes ASAP*. A one-hour seminar for several thousand PeopleSoft customers. An eight-hour seminar for the general public in Nashville the day after tomorrow. Our newest training program. An addition to our Web site.

I've worked continuously in Professional Service Firms for 25 years. I *do* projects. (Period.) I *am* my projects. (Period.)

Watch *ER*. "They" (the cast) are doing ... projects. Called patient cases. Watch professional football. For an NFL coach, there are 16 regular-season "projects" (games), up to 4 postseason projects (playoff games), 44 projects (the development of each roster player), 1 project (the season).

## Projects are me. (Tom Peters.)

## Projects are him. (San Francisco 49ers coach Steve Mariucci.)

## And projects should/can/MUST be Y-O-U! (A-n-d ttttthhhhaaaattt'sss really a-l-l, folks.)

Once more. My uncompromising, unequivocal point here: One hundred percent—no rounding error!—of "Dept." work CAN be converted to Client-centric Project Work.

"We" (PSFers) live *for* our ... Clients. We live to *do* ... projects. That's it. That's all. And if you can't convert "it" (the "mundane" task) to a Client-centric Project? Well ... drop it. Cold. Now.

1. Make it c-l-e-a-r:

"I [boss of a 2- or 22-person internal PSF] plan to make a difference. I plan for **us**—our projects, every single one—to make a difference. To **stand for** something (rather) b-i-g. There is a revolution going on. And we damn well intend to be a part of it. If not … if every one of our projects does not aim for WOW! … then why (the bloody Hell) are we doing it?"

2. Call an emergency meeting with your immediate colleagues and ask: What would we have to do to turn our "task" into a Memorable Client-centric Project? BE SPECIFIC.

# P-L-E-A-S-E.

3. Up the ante: List *everything* that *everyone* in the "Dept." is doing. (Right now.) How much of that work is Memorable Client-centric Projects? **(Be brutally honest … it is your life/lives.)**

Discuss—in detail!—every activity that is *not* a Memorable Client-centric Project.

## WHY NOT DROP IT?

(OR COMPLETELY REINVENT IT!)

# 4a.

### *The Nub*

The nub of PSF: *The work matters!* The project *is* my identity. My signature. My legacy. (For better.) (Or for worse.)

In Dilbertville (a.k.a. Cubicle Hell), life (work life) is a farce. And, God knows, I have bad days. Positively rotten days. (I don't take Prozac for yucks!) But my work matters. Or I damn well **try** to make it so. A speech to 6 people. Or 6,000. NO DIFFERENCE. It is a punctuation mark in my life. I care. And I intend for it to matter. True, 98+ percent of the 700 people who attend my seminar next Wednesday in Memphis will have forgotten about it a month from now. But for 3 or 4 of those 700 it will have come at the right personal moment ... and will have made a difference in their lives. And that means a lot to me. In fact, I'm proud as the dickens of it. And I want **(INSIST THAT?)** *you* be proud-as-all-get-out about what you do. I want what *you* do to matter.

I *intend* to matter.

I'm often disappointed.

But my *intent* is c-l-e-a-r.

I see no reason to get up in the morning if I don't mean to matter.

And: **What about you?**

## <u>WHEN MY DETERMINED ENEMY IS MY BEST FRIEND</u>

I just hung up from a half-hour call with an old nemesis. We're 20 years older than we were when we warred. Publicly. And we both have had some pretty solid successes. We are both a little annoyed at the occasional insipidity of the place where we used to toil. And that was (mostly) the subject of our exchange.

"We agreed on damn little," Dave (not his real name) said to me. "But we did, in effect, agree that we were fighting about things that mattered." I was his junior (a lot), and a Royal Pain in the Butt, he acknowledged. But in a good cause. "You believed. You cared. It mattered to you. You were willing to take me on when almost no one else was."

Though visibly at odds, the truth was that we fed off each other, and neither of our contributions would have risen to the heights it did had we not had each other to play off.

So my "nemesis" is in fact my best friend. And our "PSF" benefited immeasurably from our hearty contention.

Go figure.

1. Think about the "task" you are at work on now. **Does it matter?** (Be un-flinchingly honest. It- is-your-life.)

How can you reinvent it so that it does matter:

To you?

To your colleagues?

To your organization?

To your Client?

# 5.

## BECOME A CATALYST FOR REVOLUTION. (WHY NOT?) (WHAT ELSE?)

*The Nub*

Two little things happened to me a few months ago. Except that neither one was "little"... as I now view it.

After a public seminar I got a note from an attendee who runs her own consulting company. She said she'd changed her title from Consulting Director to... Catalyst for Revolution.

Yes!

# I was in hog heaven!

A short while later I gave a talk to several hundred "CIOs." (Chief Information Officers.) One e-mailed me a week or so after the event. Said he changed his title from CIO to... **C.E.F.R.N.S.**

Huh?

C.E.F.R.N.S.: **Chief Evangelist for Really Neat Stuff.**

Amen! (Hog Heaven redux.)

My life is worth living!

She's got it! He's got it! **Exactly!** It's what this book is about! **Exactly!** It's about shedding the skin of "Director of Human Resources." Or "CIO." And becoming a ... Catalyst for Revolution. A Chief Evangelist for Really Neat Stuff.

It's what I've dedicated my life to. It's what boosts me from bed in the morning. It's why I loved the Navy Seabees. And McKinsey ... even when I hated it.

And: It's what I hope *you* can find.

## T.T.D./C.E.F.R.N.S. (Etc.)

1. So what are you waiting for? Appoint yourself ... as of now ... and officially:

* Catalyst for Revolution

   Or:

* Chief Evangelist for Really Neat Stuff

   Or:

* Any damn title you want that expresses what you aim to accomplish in your new life as a WOW-er working for a WOW-ful PSF

2. Talk with your close colleagues about C.F.R. and C.E.F.R.N.S. and the title you've come up with for yourself. What—exactly—does each one mean? What would it mean to us collectively? To our Clients? (And: If we have problems with such language ... **WHY?**)

# II. portfolio
## quality!

# 6.

Initiate a "deep" and ongoing dialogue with ...**every**...client.

Let's get rolling. *There is only one legitimate "first step": Get out of the office—pronto!—and visit your Clients.* Off you go to *their* offices!

Start by humbly asking: "How are we doing? Are the current projects we're doing with you...Okay...or WOW? Or are we doing a half-ass job? Are we **listening** to your concerns? Do you 'love us' ... or merely 'like us' ... or, heaven forbid, 'dislike us'?"

The idea here is to start a genuine, "deep," open dialogue with every client you serve. **Now.**

### The Nub

There **IS** a "first step." Toward PSF World. And no other. It's called ... hang out ... with C-l-i-e-n-t-s.

## So ... go visit.

My pal Bob Waterman (co-author of *In Search of Excellence*) took over McKinsey & Co.'s Australian office many years ago. He began his tour of duty by ... visiting clients.

He heard some good news. And some bad news. He ended up doing over—gratis—a bunch of work that had been poorly done. The redo effort launched an enormous office comeback, the reverberations of which echo to this day, well over two decades later. We (you-me) must start this "PSF-thing"... somewhere. And the best "somewhere"— bar none!—is by undertaking systematic, Let-Down-Your-Hair Client Visitations.

## "I'm here to serve you. Period.

## "I am here to do life-altering work. Period.

## "Sooooooo ... how'm I doing?"

That's the (mendicant's) pitch ... à la Bob Waterman ... and me. HOW AM I/ARE WE DOING?

No more.

No less. (It may sound easy. It's not. Trust me. Been there. Done that. Hat-in-hand.)

And if a Client lets you have it between the eyes ... tells you the unvarnished truth about what uninspiring work you've been doing ... get down on your knees ... and THANK HER! This is manna from heaven. This is music to your ears. This is where you *learn*. This is how you *grow*. This is how you *begin* to earn your stripes as a WOW!-ing PSFer.

**1.** Make a visitation calendar: Set a date to visit—in person!—every C-l-i-e-n-t ... **in the next three weeks.**

**2.** Put together—with your colleagues—a **M**endi-cant's **Q**uestionnaire. Ask each Client: (1) How are we doing? (2) Rate us ... *mercilessly.* (3) Are we *pushing* you? (4) Are we *dazzling* you? (Use the damn word!) (5) Are we *disappointing* you?

**3.** Involve a third party—an "honest broker"—to make sure you are getting straight feedback. Remember:

# The truth alone shall start ye on the path to PSF-WOW!

# 7.

You—Dept. head turned Managing Partner of HR Inc. (Etc.)—**are** your Project List.

So … take care to construct a good one! Work with your Clients and departmental associates to create the initial list.

It's not a walk in the park, and you'll end up scuttling a bunch of your current work. But the process—and the logic behind it—are at the heart of PSF-ing, of converting your Dept. to a true-blue, rockin' Professional Service Firm.

Obviously this is an ongoing effort, but it needs to start with a bang. And a big dose of honesty. I.e.:

## Weed out the drab, the dull, the dreary…

including any number of staff and Client pet projects. You're only as good as your projects, and a weak project can drag down a whole department…um…nascent PSF!

### *The Nub*

Lists. *Two* Lists, to be precise. Client Lists. Project Lists. You—individual, "Dept." turned "PSF"—**are** those two Lists. *Period.*

Alfred A. Knopf, publisher of this book, *is* its "List" of authors and its "List" of upcoming books. *Period.* I am my list of upcoming seminars. *Period.*

So … let's take these **Lists** seriously. Very. (And, yes … I do insist on capitalizing the "L.") You and your gang of 19 in HR or Finance should:

(1) **know your Current Projects List by heart** (no kidding!);

(2) **have it on everyone's computer and posted on the wall** (the editorial support company Wordworks has a big wallboard—six feet by eight feet— with all projects listed and next steps, due dates, key responsibilities also prominently posted);

(3) **have it stuck on your fridge door at home;** and

(4) **have it tucked under your pillow** (Okay, this last one's a maybe—but a real maybe).

Section II—items No. 6 through No. 9a—is titled "Portfolio Quality!" Portfolio: Nice word. The two **Lists** are portfolios: Portfolio of Clients, Portfolio of Current Projects. Think "stock portfolio," and you think: quality, diversity, riskiness, etc. Well, I want—demand?—that you think exactly the same way about your Portfolio of

Current Projects. (Again, I apologize for the repetition. But you will be remembered by your Portfolio of Projects. Period. Right? THINK ABOUT IT. E.g., my publisher and friend Sonny Mehta will be known by the quality and originality and packaging and marketing of the titles he has published.)

## Me/You/Us/

## Budding PSF =

## Our Project List.

### T.T.D./A Stellar Project List

**1.** First things first: List *all* the projects you and your gang are working on. Big. Tiny. In between. This is easier said than done: It's *all* the "stuff" that occupies your day. Be careful, and take pains as you do this.

**2.** Start a file—**with a file number**—for each project.

**3.** Now start (this is the Main Game) the evaluation process: Score *each* project quantitatively on dimensions such as WOW!, Excitement, Urgency, Impact. And don't limit yourself to my list; add whatever dimensions apply to a specific project. (Spend a *lot* of time on this. Please. Again: This *is* you. And yours. Truly.)

**4.** Get trusted/interesting outsiders involved in the evaluation process.

**5.** Once you've mulled this over quite a bit, take it to your Clients. In a very open-ended, hair-down session,

have them review **The List** and the evaluations. E.g.:
"Given our [PSF] limited resources ... is this the best-of-all-possible Lists?" "Is there enough 'Seriously Cool' stuff on this List?" "What should we dump?"

## (ANSWER: WE SHOULD PROBABLY "DUMP" 75 PERCENT OF IT. SERIOUSLY!?)

# 8.

I.e.: What does your "project list"/"project portfolio" *add up to*? Is it exciting? (How exciting?) Is it bland?

## You—newly minted PSF Managing Partner—are nothing more (or less) than a bettor-on-projects.

### *The Nub*

I groove on imagery! Metaphors! A V.C./Venture Capital firm is, of course, a "real" PSF. But it is also the perfect metaphor for **any** PSF.

What does a VC do? Bets on people. Bets on Projects. Period. Right?

And that's exactly what a "real" PSF does. The adman David Ogilvy said that his firm does only two things: (1) services clients and (2) develops advertising talent.

## Amen!

That's "all."

## Service Clients.

# Develop Talent.

## And your vehicle: projects. (WOW Projects… we hope.)

Computer visionary Michael Dell has said what we all know: Deciding what to do is easy. Deciding what **not** to do is the hard part, the art. So, too, Ms./Mr. PSF. Deciding what is **not** IDEO, what projects are **not** us … that's the magical act!

So … think venture capitalist. You-are-one!

T.T.D. / "Getting" V.C.-World

1. What *is* my "Firm"? (PSF.)

*Answer:*

## Our Talent. Our Clients. Our Projects.

Hence: Make, for starters, a careful inventory of each. Okay, I've asked that before. Perhaps you're getting the point by now?! (So … have you done it yet?)

2. V.C.s spread their risks. Some projects they bet on are more or less sure things. Some are long shots (with potentially stratospheric payoffs). Is our PSF Portfolio like that: Have we got a few "important" surefire winners? And some "long shots" that could change our and our Clients' lives? (Read closely: CHANGE OUR AND OUR CLIENTS' LIVES. Stiff test, eh?)

3. Invite a local V.C. in for a Brown Bag Lunch. Ask her/him to talk about V.C.-life … and thence your life.

What are her decision criteria? How does she decide when to bail out? What is *the* single most important thing she looks for in a company (a.k.a. a project?). What raises a red flag and causes her to turn and run? Last, how would she evaluate your (PSF) portfolios of talent, Clients, projects? As always: brutal honesty, please. (And: Invite her/him to be your formal adviser? Hmmmmm?!)

# 9.

## The Project-List-is-us. So ... now we've got to start managing the Hell out of it!

Post the list. Electronically. Put it up on butcher paper on the wall ... or on an oversized white board. Bring the list to life! Talk it up. Use it as the basis for big(gish) weekly reviews.

### The Nub

PUT PROJECTS—**AND THE STATUS THEREOF**—AT THE TOP OF YOUR VISIBLE AGENDA.

If Projects-Are-Me, then reviewing those projects' status is of paramount importance. So ... let's get serious. Let's have a Current Projects Review ... at least weekly. **Maybe ... daily?**

A few years ago I visited CNN headquarters in Atlanta. Every morning at about seven o'clock, the big-wigs got together for 30 minutes max. All the world's bureau chiefs were there via conference call. All had in hand a white-hot document, just minutes old, that laid out the day … as they then knew it.

In short order, that day was discussed, dissected—no holds barred. What's good? (Or not?) What stories may break? (Or not?) Etc.

CNN-*is*-its-projects. Projects = Stories (shows, news, etc.) The "portfolio" is the on-air day. (Twenty-four hours a day … forever.) The meeting is of the utmost importance. It focuses everyone on the day/projects/portfolio/milestones/overall "look" of what's immediately ahead. It also puts everyone squarely on the same page (never, *ever* assume people know what's going on outside their own bailiwicks), and it prepares people for potential surprises. The meeting is also a forum for airing problems and finding solutions. And it's a great morale booster, a chance for folks to vent, bond, and … God forbid! … introduce a little levity into the workday.

We're not all in CNN's business. So maybe daily-at-7:00 a.m. is somewhat over the top. The idea surely isn't: It's the premier way of getting people to focus on … projects … **projects** … **projects.**

Hence: Invent your own version. But don't stray too far from that CNN model. (If you're smart.)

## T.T.D./Current Projects Review

1. Bring projects and project status to (vivid) life. Somehow. My suggestion (command?): Schedule a weekly

(or daily, if it makes sense … which it well may) review. At a specific time. Involve out-of-the-office types.

2. Goal: We are trying to make WOW Projects the centerpiece of our daily affairs. So the dialogue is: Where are we on the Project? … What's new and next? … What's Cool (and un-Cool)? … Etc.

3. **YOU GOTTA DO THIS. SOMEHOW. OR OTHER. OKAY?**

## WORDS . . . MATTER.
## E.G.: "ENGAGEMENT."

### *The Nub*

McKinsey & Co. does not—in fact—do "projects." The Firm (don't forget the capital letters!) does Engagements (don't forget the capital letter) with Clients (don't forget the capital letter).

E.g.:
* **T**he **F**irm
* **E**ngagements
* **C**lients

Okay? Is it really that simple? (And are the capital letters really that important?)

**Yes.**

The company is the **F**irm. The customer is the **C**lient. And the project is the **E**ngagement. E-n-g-a-g-e-s: It's a proactive joint venture in which the rather talented boys and girls of McKinsey join with their partner-Clients to closely examine an intractable problem. (Intractable, because if the damn thing wasn't intractable, why pay McKinsey's astonishingly high fees? But, hey, life is not worth living unless you are at work on intractable problems. Eh?)

Engagement. Event. **Happening.** Cool Shit. Memorable Experience. Adventure. **Journey.**

All these words come to mind ... which is precisely the point. This *are* us! These *are* what *we* do. The Engagements. Happenings. Stuff we might still be bragging about ... 10 **(20!?)** years from now. Okay?

T.T.D./"Engagements"

1. Is each "project" a

# H-A-P-P-E-N-I-N-G?

(At least potentially so?) (Think about it.) Can you label it—à la McKinsey—an **E**ngagement? Or: An **E**vent? An **A**dventure?

2. Look anew at that Current Projects List and evaluate each one in Engagement/Event/Happening terms. PLEASE.

3. WHAT E-L-S-E IS THERE? **(No kidding.)**

# III. impact!

# 10.

There are projects…and then there are projects. Remember: Projects-Are-You. So, you damn well better make 'em memorable. My advice:

## Use the WOW! Scale. (Literally.)

## "Measure" every project on a 1 to 10 WOW!-O-Meter.

For example, a prestigious headhunter pal went to each of her current clients and asked: "What would a 'WOW!' result for this Search look like?" In other words, not an "okay" result, not a "good" result, not even an "excellent" result, but a WOW!/Cool/High Impact/Transformative result. She reports a major shift in emphasis in several cases … *and* those memorable results … thanks simply to the use of WOW-language per se.

### *The Nub*

It was a little thing. *V-e-r-y* little. Redesign a reporting format…for a mostly unread report…in the Pentagon in 1968. I always liked statistics. And I decided Why Not? (Perhaps boredom!) I decided I'd take the little assignment seriously. So I labored over it.

To my surprise, some people v-e-r-y senior to me began to discuss the results of the redesigned and beefed-up document. And I decided this could be a hoot. (Best sense of that word.)

A year—and a dozen monthly iterations and refinements—later a large number of field operations were, in effect, being principally evaluated by my "little report."

Lesson I: The "little" report revision became … in the parlance I now use … a WOW! Project. Lesson II (and this took much longer to learn): There are no non-WOW! Projects … **if** … you put your mind to it. The most trivial task can be turned into Something Very Cool … something that has Impact. An actor pal tells me there's a saying in his trade: **"There are no small parts, only small actors."** To which I would add: "There are no small tasks, only small imaginations."

It's a lesson I haven't forgotten. And now I intend to pass it along. In short:

## Non-WOW! = No-no.

Okay?

So … like our headhunter friend above … ask each and every client: **"How could we WOW!-the-Hell out of this project?"** (Use the word! Practice using it! Start now! Okay? W-O-W! As in … W-O-W!)

1. Call one Client n-o-w. Mention your current project. Use *my* language:

**"So, on a scale of 1 to 10, where 1 is 'Insipid' and 10 is 'WOW!' ... how ... *exactly* ... would you rate our current project?"**

(P-l-e-a-s-e: Do consider my *exact* language. Or some very close variant thereto.)

2. **Put "WOW!" in the language!** One client reports that, following my merciless goading, everybody in her Finance Dept. is asking, "But is it a real 'WOW!'?" Love that! (I have become a fanatic on the subject: "IS IT 'WOW!'?" is my constant refrain. Ask my poor suffering colleagues!)

3. **Apply—now!—the WOW! Test to the most *trivial* (seemingly) activity you are working on.** Again: A-n-y-t-h-i-n-g can be WOW!-ed up. Agree? (And if you don't, discuss it ... ASAP ... with your colleagues. And your shrink.)

# 11.

## NEVER EVER
## COMPROMISE YOUR IDENTITY.

**(P.S.: WHAT IS YOUR IDENTITY?)**

**(Apple knows. BMW knows. Why not you?)**

**(Damn it.)**

So ... *WHO ARE YOU, ANYWAY?* "HR Dept." (Bad/worst answer.) "HR Inc." (Not much better.) My question: *What are you up to ... that's Distinguished? How are you Special ... e.g., Different from 100 other "HR Depts."?*

Some suggest you should be able to state your "position" in ... **8** words. Others will give you 35 words.

My position on position: You'd better have a P-o-s-i-t-i-o-n! And I know darn few "Depts." that do ... and, for that matter, not so many "real" PSFs that do either.

To start: Mount a serious dialogue around Position/ Identity. Now. (Why wait?)

# WHAT IS
# OUR POINT OF VIEW?

### *The Nub*

"Identity." "Brand." "Stand for." Words we associate with Coke, Pepsi, Nike, The Gap. Martha Stewart. Calvin Klein. Tina Brown.

But our "HR Department"? Don't be silly, you say. And … **WHY** (the Hell) **NOT!?** … I answer.

Don't you want to be the Coke-Nike of HR "Departments." (Or PSFs, per me)?

It may be arrogance. (I don't think so.) Or ego. (I don't think so.) But I want to **stand for s-o-m-e-t-h-i-n-g.** I'm not willing to leave "stand for" to Coke or Martha S.

How about *you*?

When we say "Purchasing Dept.," even at IBM or Nike, the words "stand for" don't immediately come to mind. And I think that's an **(egregious)** mistake. I think our Training (Purchasing, etc.) "Dept."—or PSF—ought to be as cool as Nike … or McKinsey … or Arthur Andersen … or IDEO.

# Why not?

Thence: PSF-ism, per me, is all about … Distinction … Signature … Point of View … Identity. Different ad agencies have different reputations (Kinky, Reliable, Boring, etc.). So, too, consultancies … and accountancies … and law firms … and architects.

So ... why not you?

# P-L-E-A-S-E.

**1. WHO ARE WE?** With apologies to Hamlet, *that* is the question. When was the last time you asked ... or thought about it? Start now. As in ... t-o-d-a-y. Sit with two or three colleagues at lunch and launch, informally, the Who-Are-We-Discussion.

**2.** What ... very specifically ... do we stand for? What is our Credo? Start this discussion ... ASAP. How do we— again, specifically?—stand out from the crowd? A local (let alone national) architect must stand for something ... have a distinctive personality ... a style, a look, a way of working with Clients she's known for; so, too, must a law firm. So ... why not us? **(Damn it!?)**

# 12.

"Energetic purchasing organization": That has a nice ring to it! Eh?

## The basic idea of PSF-ing:
## Purchasing/Finance/HR/
## Whatever ain't boring!

In fact, it is—or **should be**—a hotbed of Exciting-Value-Added-Through-Intellectual-Capital-Accumulation.

Which is to say that Passion has a place—center stage—in the "Staff Depts." (Which are now, of course, per this book, **S**cintillating **PSF**s.) Staff Depts.—*every* Staff Dept.—ought to be a **"super cool"/ "fly-phat"** place to work. I mean: WHY THE BLOODY HELL NOT?

### *The Nub*

This is ... **COOL STUFF**... we do!

It also happens to be ... **Important.**

Okay ... you agree. SO WHAT? The "So what" is ...

# P-A-S-S-I-O-N.

Passion in ... *Finance*. Passion in ... *HR*. Passion in ... *IS*. Passion in ... *Purchasing*.

I think what you do (and I do, not so incidentally) is r-o-c-k-i-n'. I think at our best ... **We Matter.** I think at our best ... **We Make a Difference.** As much as Mark McGwire. Or John Elway. Or ...?

The (other) way of putting it: **I'm sick-and-deathly-tired-of the passion-less-ness with which HR ... and IS ... and Finance ... and Purchasing ... are typically viewed.**

What *I* do is cool. (At its best.) **You, too.** So, let's take the hairshirt off and own up to the rockin' potential of What We Do. (Passionately. Okay?)

**T.T.D./** Cut the Crap:
It's P-a-s-s-i-o-n Time!

1. **What's "rockin'" about what you do?** Why does it Matter? Think ... clearly ... and precisely ... about this. Make a List. Now!

2. Take your current project. Are you passionate about it? (Use the term ... **p-a-s-s-i-o-n-a-t-e.** Damn it!) If so ... why? If not ... WHY NOT? And, if not, what

—Specifically and Precisely and Now—can you do to up the Passion Score?

**3.** Step back. Gather three colleagues. What does "passion-in-accounting" (etc.) mean? P-l-e-a-s-e redux: Take this seriously. Discuss. **Now.** Urgently. At length.

# 13.

You're in this—with your Client and Project Portfolio —for the long haul. Right? So, do we know how we're doing?

*Ask!* Pick a handful of Core Clients ... no more than two ... and beg them for a full day of their time. (Yes, beg.) *After thorough preparation, work to determine if your projects with them have made a ... LASTING IMPRESSION.*

That's what this game—in the end—is all about: Is the Client in a noticeably different place/space ... because of the work you did together? THERE IS NO OTHER QUESTION! (*If* you are a committed, determined professional.)

## The Nub

"Okay." Or, rather, "Enough," you say. But I say: Never!

That is ... **I-M-P-A-C-T.** No issue—none!—is more important.

It has nothing to do with "inept leadership." I.e.: some distant "they."

It has everything to do with ... **YOU.** ME. **OUR ... ESSENCE.**

Did "it" have Impact? We exist, as I see it, to Make a Difference. (Or at least to die trying.)

I read a lot of books about Arctic and Antarctic exploration. *Endurance. The Worst Journey in the World.* I watch television shows like … *ER* … or *NYPD.* What do awesome exploration and rockin' TV shows have in common? They are all about WOW Projects … Journeys and Cases that Make a Difference to our fellow humans. Right? (And is what we're doing in "HR" less important? I don't think so.)

### T.T.D./Impact!

1. So: *Does* the current project *matter*? If not …
# Why Not?

2. How—specifically—do we raise the **I**mpact **S**core of the current project? You know exactly what I mean. Correct? So … Go for It! (Okay?)

3. Use the word. I-M-P-A-C-T. Continually.


# ( P l e a s e . )

# 14.

We dot all the "i's." We cross all the "t's." We will move heaven and earth to finish on time. And on budget. *But* that ain't . . . nearly . . . enough.

## The pressing question: Was it far enough out? Was it—Our Work—as "crazy" as these (clearly) crazy times demand?

I hold in the utmost contempt a "thoroughly professional job" . . . that does not live up to the striking demands of the times. That's my standard. None other. Ready to sign on?

### The Nub

**"But surely 'budget' matters,"** a seminar participant exclaimed to me in some frustration.

Yes! **Of course!** (I run a couple of small businesses. Budget jolly well does matter.)

Still . . .

**Was Einstein "on budget" for his research?** Or Churchill ... or Roosevelt ... for World War II? Who knows? Or cares?

Button-down management *is* imperative. But "button-down management" is an enabler ... *not* the be-all and the end-all. (As most "project management" literature would have it.)

The be-all and the end-all:

# Prov-o-damn-cation!

"If nobody's pissed at you, you're brain-dead and just haven't figured it out," snorts a friend and legendary high-tech project manager.

Projects that make a difference Provoke. Just ask Galileo, tried by the Catholic Church; Dr. Martin Luther King, Jr., assassinated; or most any other character whose life is worth mention in your tenth-grade daughter's history book.

## Not many serious social change agents avoided jail. Not many Arctic explorers came home without frost-destroyed appendages (if they came home at all).

"Provoking" doesn't mean gratuitously insulting others. It *does* mean living — permanently!—in the *dis*comfort zone ... seeking solace mostly from your Fellow WOW Project Zealots.

This logic takes on added meaning today: These are, to put it mildly, provocative times. And I contend: **Provocative Times call for Provocative Approaches.** The whole idea of "PSF" is, after all, that "normal departmental doings" are, literally, doomed. The PSF aims to Matter. Period.

## T.T.D./ Provoke!

1. Talk with your colleagues about the Year 2000 ... and what the new millennium will look like. Call in a few Wild Hares to chat with your group. Clip and distribute provocative articles (or download them from the Web). Then measure your efforts—your entire project portfolio!—against The Year 2000 Standard. **Are we in the hunt?** Or not?

2. Millennium redux. Millennial shifts only come every 1,000 years. (You heard it here first!) I view the Millennial Transformation as having unimaginable symbolic impact. My motto: **IF NOT NOW ... WHEN?** And I urge my motto on your Dept.-turned-PSF. "If not now ... when?" Put it on—no joke—your weekly review meeting's agenda. Every week. DON'T BLOW THIS ONE! (If you do, you'll have to wait another 1,000 years.)

3. Use my terms: Do all—all, every one!—of the Projects in your PSF Portfolio ... **Provoke?** Aim to Alter the Status Quo? Live up to the Millennial Challenge? Measure this. Repeatedly. (If not now, **W-H-E-N?**)

# 15.

## We are paid to lead our Clients.

PSFs are *the* primary sources of Intellectual Capital Creation ... in a world where intellectual-capital-is-all. Therefore ... PSFs are in the ... leadership business. (Or else.) So ... are *you*? *Prove it!*

### The Nub

**PSFs ARE IN THE LEADERSHIP BUSINESS. (That's the animating idea behind this book.)** And so must *you* be.

Why shift from follower-mode "Dept." to leadership-mode "PSF"? Well ...

* To save our skins in the face of the White Collar Revolution. (Never underestimate the power of self-interest.)

* Because we care.

* Because it matters.

* Because we have innovative approaches to the Client's problem and innovative rebels to help implement those approaches.

* Because it's a Helluva lot more challenging, exciting, rewarding, and FUN!

* Because we are sick-and-tired of being **"The Dull and Dreary Accounting Department"** ... the bloody "Beancounters from Hell." (Remember my take on it: ACCOUNTING ROCKS!)

Repeat after me:

# It is the new millennium!

# I am a proud professional!

# I will l-e-a-d my Clients to the Promised Land. Or burst trying.

Yes, to a large degree it's all about imagery. **The Imagery of Leadership.** It's "cool" to work at Arthur Andersen or Andersen Consulting. It's dull to work in the "Acctg. Dept." Or the "IS Dept." Why?

Why? Because we have allowed it to be so. Because, more often than not, we have **not** accepted the Leadership Challenge! We are **not** integral to our Clients' lives. We are **not** Freaky-Cool-Provocative to be around. We are **not** on a Holy Mission. We are **not** providing wildly innovative, proactive solutions. We are **not** staying five steps ahead of the game. We are **not** routinely taking risks. We are **not** inventing the future ... and then leading our Clients into it.

Well, let's change that. And let's start ... now.

1. Review the early advice about Visiting Clients. So … now … formally … revisit "lead" Clients … in the next six weeks. **The (sole) topic: ADVENTURE!** Are we on a Joint Adventure? Are we "out front"? Is our work Annoyingly Provocative (see above)? Are you scared? (If not, why not? Anyone in his/her right mind—that is, fully engaged in a worthy millennial pursuit—would be.)

2. Schedule a seminar series. Invite outsiders in your discipline to speak. Invite clients to the Series.

## Convert your Dept.-turned-PSF into a highly visible Hotbed of Provocative Ideas.

## Become a Shop of Thought Leaders.

## A Place to Be.

Consider push e-mails to clients in which you offer provocative vignettes about things of importance.

3. Ask at every Weekly Projects Review: Are we **(t-r-u-l-y)** pushing/leading/goading the Client? Put it in your quarterly evaluation criteria set. (Don't screw around with this!)

# 16.

PSF mantra:

**We are not scornful of the grubby "politics of getting things done." We Embrace Them as the *sine qua non* of effective implementation.**

Deloitte & Touche pride themselves on being...*boring.* I.e.: highly effective. Their solutions work in the real world. Implementation Excellence is their (very potent) "identity." The point: Making sure that "things get done" and that yours is not just one-more-consultant's-report-gathering-dust-on-the-shelf. A lot of PSFs—sad to say—turn up their noses at "client politics."

FOR SHAME! Politics—mutual accommodation—is life. Yes: Stay prickly. Stick to your (noisy) guns. But ... understand that you're also part of the hurly-burly of real life. Implementation often (always?) requires compromise. There's no effective CEO who has not had to resort to "politics" upon many an occasion. The same is true for successful PSFs.

So ... join the club. AND ... WELCOME TO THE REAL WORLD!

*The Nub*

WORK THAT COUNTS GETS IMPLEMENTED. IT'S THAT SIMPLE.

AND, UH: IMPLEMENTATION EFFECTIVENESS = POLITICAL SAVVY. (THE EMBRACE THEREOF.)

Politics ... a **lovely** word. Politics ... the Art of Getting Things Done. Does principle matter? Absolutely I. Does politics matter? Absolutely II. Are the two mutually exclusive? **No!** Does balancing principles and politics routinely require the acrobatic skills of a tightrope walker? **Yes!** Are these skills that the successful PSFer *must* develop? **Yes, yes, yes!**

My personal PSF experience has been that about **80** percent of my time is spent on ... politics. Call it sales. Call it compromise. Call it schmoozing. Call it creating grubby implementation plans. Call it working with the frontline grunts—in Toledo or Timbuktu—who are essential to the implementation of my "clever" scheme. Call it: P-o-l-i-t-i-c-s!

Did you read what I just wrote? **Eighty percent of my time.** That's a big fat chunk. It is a privilege to be writing this book. It is as pure an expression of creativity as I can muster. And it is but the tiniest tip of the Tom Peters iceberg. Any impact I've made over the years has come from the fact that the (infrequent) books have been augmented by hundreds of seminars (and thousands of hours waiting for delayed flights), by hundreds (perhaps thousands) of press interviews, by hundreds of one-on-one meetings to thrash out seemingly small (but highly significant) details of some event. Etc. Etc. Etc.

Fact is, I enjoy the seminars, the feedback, the challenging questions, the media sideshow, the one-on-ones, the down-in-the-trenches toil. (Though I can't say I enjoy the flight delays.) I enjoy it because I know it's *essential* to my work's having impact…and I want to know I'm having impact. Like me, the consummate PSFers enjoy—thrive on!—The Politics of Implementation. It's not a "distraction." It's the **Main Game** … in the long haul.

It's a fascinating phenomenon: That young PSFer who thinks the clever solution—tossed off like a brilliant jewel—is the be-all and end-all. Ah, the arrogance (and ignorance) of youth. (But bless her … we desperately need her cleverness and fearlessness.) But the PSFer who triumphs in the long haul … who gets promoted to the top ranks…quickly learns that The Politics of Lasting Impact is the only road to creation of a legacy that sticks.

## T.T.D./ The (Joyous) Politics of Implementation

**1.** Back we (you) go again to … the … Client. This time: Perform a gloves-off Impact Review. *"Did our stuff stick?" "When did it fail to stick?" "Why did it fail to stick?"* Conduct—at least—an Annual Impact Review with every core client.

**2.** Is Implementation (the politics thereof) a prime project consideration from Day No. 1? (Are you sure?)

Stop.

Schedule an **I**mplementation **R**eview ... of every project. (In the next two weeks.)

**3.** How clear/predominant is Implementation Effectiveness in the core values of the PSF? And in everyone's **Formal Evaluation**?

**4.** Are frontline members of the Client organization on *every* project team? (Hint: They ought to be if you're serious about implementation!)

**5.** Does every project include a clear, formal Implementation Plan? And do you begin working on that plan at the **start** of the project?

**6.** Are you training in project implementation? Do you openly discuss the **Politics of implementation**?

**7.** PSF chief:

Have you **fired** (yes!) anyone in the PSF because of lousy implementation skills? (If not, you are kidding yourself about implementation's importance. Trust me.)

# 17.

You want to be Provocative. Amen. And ... you want to make a Difference. (Actually have *something happen* because of your efforts!) Amen. Hence, it's all a grand and glorious juggling act.

### The Nub

Cool = Cool. Implementation = Impact. And never the twain shall meet ... precisely.

Push. Prod. Provoke. **And** ... implement. Lead the client. **And** ... write the **D**efinitive **D**etailed **I**mplementation **M**anual.

I'm angry. Twice over. Angry that damn few "Depts."— and not all that many PSFs, truth be told—meet my Millennial Provocation Standard. *And* I'm also angry that so many PSFs are piss-poor implementers, who ignore the Client's frontline players. Who bridle at writing the 200-page implementation manual and then conducting the training for **40,000 (or 400)** folks to breathe life into that manual.

Bottom line: Life is about the fine art of balance. Life is a juggling act. Juggling your work ... and your family ...

and your friends ... and your extracurricular passions and ... whatever. It's about balancing your needs and dreams and aspirations ... with what you can actually accomplish. Those who do it successfully have mastered the art of living. So it should come as no surprise that **the great PSF**—which is what I demand that your "Dept." become!—is beset perpetually with artistic issues.

Excitement. Verve. Cool. **Rockin' freaks.** And ... **GETTING IT DONE.** You *need* both. And there is no simple, pat way to have both. Many PSFs veer from being too conservative to being too radical. The Conservatives flunk the WOW! Test. The Radicals flunk the Implementation Test.

Believe me, there is no easy or definitive answer. "Do both" is about as useful as saying, "Be tall and be short." Not in this lifetime.

*Worry* about both? Yes! *Focus* on both? Yes! But "be" both? Never! It's clear: Some (good) PSFs are known for radical work. Some (good) PSFs are known for implementation excellence. Few (none?) are known for "excellence" at both simultaneously.

**So you juggle.** You lean left. You lean right. You obsess about both issues. But "get it right"? Not going to happen. That does not, however (HUGE "HOWEVER"), mean you can stop trying for even an instant! If you do, your balance will surely flip out of whack and you'll be in big trouble—either full of useless WOW! (you can't put it into practice) or toothless implementation (your solutions are mediocre at best).

### 1. Talk loudly out of both sides of your mouth at the same time!

Talk "cool." Talk "implementation excellence." Keep both (permanently) on the front burners. And never let either "dish" overcook while the other stays raw.

**2.** *Formalize* the talk (of No. 1 above). Measure—qualitatively—effectiveness on both dimensions. Cool Scale. Implementation Scale.

**3.** Hire (and promote) with both "sides" in mind. Which almost invariably means two different kinds of people. Don't waste your time on a fruitless search for nirvana—both skills in one individual. This supersoul may exist somewhere … but I've yet to meet her (and I've been around the block a few times).

**4.** Sign up for a series of classes in juggling and tightrope walking. (I'm more or less serious about this.)

# 18.

### The Nub

I *am* on a mission! I freely admit it. HR is Cool! Accounting Rocks! IS is Phat! At least as cool-rockin'-phat as anything that happens on a football field or on the stage.

So Mr./Ms. HR-Accountant, I want you to start thinking like John Elway or Gwyneth Paltrow or Luciano Pavarotti or Robin Williams ... or Your-Favorite-Performer. You are a ... performing artist.

## (You perform WOW Projects that could make thousands of lives—for peers, customers—better. **Right?**)

Performing artists draw upon one thing above all others: their unique natural talents. And, praise be, *everyone* has unique natural talents! What are *yours*? Are you using them *fully* at work? Come on, colleagues, that's what it's all about. *You!* **Fabulous, glorious, gifted you!** (I'm not living in a dreamland. I know not everyone can be a superstar. But I also know—*with every fiber of my being*—that *everyone* has untapped reservoirs of talent. At its core, this book is about creating a place—**Rockin' PSF**—where you can unabashedly find and unleash *your* gifts.)

It's personal! I **love** PSF-land! Ad agency-land! Law firm-land! Graphic design-land! Architecture-land! Accountancy-land! Publishing-land! Web-land! Consultancy-land! HR-land! IS-land!

I love it because it is/can be about human creativity and problem solving.(Especially now that computers are starting to do so much of the rote, "dirty white collar" work.) I love it because it's about invention. I love it because it's about Hot Teams. That is, I love my PSF life because it is a performing art! And I want you to love yours.

### T.T.D./ Performing Art—Performing Artist

1. **Are we having fun yet?** (No joke!) PSF chief: What have you done ... **today** ... to turn "all this" into a "Millennial Adventure?" A safari? An extravaganza? A championship game? Think about it. Carefully. Please.

2. Be tacky! **Fill the walls with adventure posters, movie posters, sports star poses.**

(Or some such.) Have an explorer come to talk to your group ... an entertainer ... the producer of a Vegas show ... a magician ... a whoever-will-inspire your nascent stars to new heights! Think P-E-P! Think P-A-S-S-I-O-N! Think P-E-R-F-O-R-M-A-N-C-E!

# 19.

### The Nub

And now a word from our sponsor! A PSF is also a . . . **b-u-s-i-n-e-s-s.** We want our "associates" to focus on high-impact WOW Projects. We want them to be slaves to their Clients. We also want them to think like entrepreneurs . . . and first-rate product developers. (PSFs are exactly as good as the new products they're adding to their portfolios.) But we also want (and need) them to be shrewd about budgets and timelines. And expense management.

No, you (I!) don't have to be equally good at "*all* this stuff." But "business stuff" must exist at the preconscious level every day for every one of us career PSFers.

Some PSFs—no names will be mentioned—worry so much about professionals' percentage of billable hours ("utilization") that WOW! fades into the horizon. I think that stinks! On the (important) other hand . . .

it is imperative that all of us full well realize that we must perform **"services worth paying for."**

The solution: Keep at least one eye half-focused on the bottom line. Pavarotti, for all his artistry, does. And so, too, must Jane Smith in Accounting ... and, by the way, Tom Peters.

### T.T.D./Businesspersons All!

**1.** PSF chief: Explain the "business model" to your colleagues. What we charge. What it costs to do business. It need not be (best not be!) complicated, but it should be clear. I.e.:

# Make everyone a conscious co-conspirator in the drive to do ... Work Worth Paying For!

**2.** Give everyone a simple summary of the Monthly Financials. (Even if you don't make the formal decision to become a PSF.) Have a monthly or bimonthly lunch at which you discuss the financials. (Provide appropriate training as well; everyone should be up to speed on business-financial basics.) The point here is to make the whole crew aware of what's at stake (a.k.a. their jobs!).

**3.** Work with each PSF member on a Business Plan. **(Call it that!)** This replaces MBO (Management by Objectives) or whatever your current evaluation process features.

# 20.

A few projects that scare you? Okay, I just gave my blessing to politics. And profits. (Ah ... life.) But back to that totally defining portfolio of projects:

**If you want some "great stuff" to happen ... well ... you have absolutely no alternative: Your portfolio has to include some Truly Freaky Stuff.**

### The Nub

Why do you think Silicon Valley is the Economic Center of the Universe? Sure, it's got Hewlett-Packard. No small thing. But it's also spawned its (un)fair share of Apples and Yahoos and Oracles and Intuits and Ciscos— the freakish results of lots of freaky tries. (Freaks trying freaky stuff ... to extend the use of my favorite word.) Or "insanely great" outcomes, to steal from Apple's Steve Jobs, which result only from ... lotsa insane "bets." Made without a safety net!

## No long shots.

## No breakthroughs.

Could it be that simple? No. But close.

**Perhaps it's my No. 1 problem with "depts.": the "line extension" syndrome.** Most projects are variations on current themes. Damn few are leaps in the dark. And yet to get that occasional home run (or even a triple), you've got to be willing to try things—lots of!—you've never dared try before.

## "THE GOOD LOSS"

Jon Katzenbach, my subsequent mentor, became Managing Director of a sound but uninspiring McKinsey & Co. office in San Francisco in 1970. He and his partners were determined to change their stuffy image ... and have more fun. They began to bid on exciting business. And suggest bold approaches to sometimes stuffy Clients.

Often as not, the Clients didn't buy the act. This didn't deter Katzenbach et al. In fact, they developed a name for these rejections: "the good loss." A good loss was a noble effort—perhaps ahead of its time—that, even though it didn't pay off, was consistent with the larger aspirations of the San Francisco partner group.

Over time, the wins began to roll in and the office's project portfolio became edgier and edgier. By the time I arrived a few years later, McKinsey's San Francisco office was the Hottest Spot—people and projects—in the entire company. To this day, Jon Katzenbach attributes the turnaround to "the good loss" idea.

**1.** *This could be the most important "T.T.D." in the book:*

# Evaluate **every** project in your portfolio. Now. On riskiness.

How many are long-odds bets on, say, Cool Technology or Freaky-Cool People? My dictum: If 25 percent of your portfolio isn't made up of risky/wild/freaky projects … then the odds against "hitting one out of the park" are almost impossibly high. (Please think deeply—and collectively—about this.)

**2.** Invite in a trusted—and somewhat "freaky"—outsider to evaluate your full project portfolio. On a scale of 1 to 10 (1 = cautious; 10 = wild *and* woolly), how many of your projects does she rate as a 7, 8, 9, or 10? Then pick her brain about how to increase that number … and/or prune the total number while increasing the scores of those that remain.

**3.** Examine/re-examine *every* current project: How can you up the Wild and Woolly Score on "even" the smallest of them? Hint: My experience is it can be done. And in fact, the "smallest of them" is the best starting place. Small projects usually have lots of "play room," precisely because they are small and therefore not subject to microscopic scrutiny by "the suits."

**4.** In the next month, take on one freaky project that basically scares the bejesus out of you.

(In fact, use your degree of fright to measure the worthiness of the project.)

Go into it knowing full well it might fail—and equally full well that it just might be a grand slam. I'm serious about this: It's the ultimate real-world test of your commitment.

## Think of it as an Outward Bound exercise for would-be PSFers.

# 21.

It's arrogant. It's egocentric. But it's the "measure" you'd best have in mind. Question to ask yourself:

## "WHAT—IF ANYTHING—WILL MY THREE YEARS AS MANAGING PARTNER OF PURCHASING INC. BE REMEMBERED FOR?"

### *The Nub*

Think back on your three years in the Omaha Distribution Center … 11 years ago. I bet there's but one (big) thing that really stands out: "We really got the EDI [Electronic Data Interchange] program humming!" Or whatever.

## The typical job stint, in 9 cases out of 10, is remembered for o-n-e thing.

One prays it's a wondrous thing that made a difference … your Signature for those 2-3-4 *years* of your life. That makes it one **b-i-g** deal, eh?

I beseech you to think more purposefully and proactively about legacy. As PSF chief, say, you've got 19 people working for you in Purchasing (HR, etc.); and as we speak, they are at work on seven projects. So: What do those projects (potentially) add up to? Are they tasks served up on a platter by "top management" ... performed by you with "all due diligence"? Or did you take what was handed you and look at it from a new PSF–P.O.V. That is, enhance it with, for example, an e-commerce angle, because that's really where you want your Signature to be?

Winners focus! **PSF winners focus insanely!** To some extent, you have to accept what's dished up ... but the determined focuser will—per the above—make sure that most every project reflects the place she/he wants to make a dramatic impact.

Hey ... only three years to the assignment. Not a moment to waste! (Some U.S. presidents have handed out "backwards" calendars to their staff ... counting down the number of days left in the current term of office. Not a bad idea for you to appropriate.)

**T.T.D./Focus-Legacy**

1. This is personal!

What is the prospective
# Signature
of your three-year
Adventure in Purchasing?

What—very succinctly—do you want the tour of duty to be remembered for? **Write it down. One para-**

**graph.** (Your first guess may be dead wrong ... but you need to be thinking this way ... **ASAP.**)

2. Assuming you've got some notion of what you want your mark to be, have you managed to install this bias (point of view) into every/damn-near-every project in the PSF's portfolio?

3. Bring in cool-prestigious outsiders to talk to the gang about stuff that starts to reinforce/infuse this "main idea" bias into the unit-PSF.

4. Search out "cool"—though perhaps rather officially powerless—Clients who will partner with you in wild and woolly experiments, which explore your **M**ain **I**dea.

# **22.**

## PITCH IN . . .
## OR BAIL OUT!

The "Project Life" cries out for unstinting mutual support. Gary Withers, chief of Imagination, Britain's zany marketing services firm, is as big a fan of WOW! as you'll find anywhere.

But he insists that *the* key to his success is that anybody at any level—no matter how busy she is!—will drop what she's doing and help out anyone else in a pinch.

That is, Great PSFs are about exceptional vision *and* an unstinting commitment to one another, a frown-free willingness to jump in when the going gets tough for somebody else. And the going often does get tough . . . if you stand for something worthwhile/a little far out.

### *The Nub*

Project! Focus! Commitment! All true.

## AND . . . mutual support.

My old employers McKinsey & Co. demanded a singularity of project focus that addicted me to Tylenol and Mylanta (not to mention caffeine). The mantra was: The project. The project. The bloody damn project.

# But…

There was an **(enormous)** exception. If a colleague called from Australia or Austria … and needed info. Or if a project team needed a hand at 11:00 p.m., the day before a presentation … well, you dropped what you were doing and lent that hand. Or you were history.

I'm not sure there was much altruism to it, frankly. It was more that you knew for sure you'd be in the same pinch … time and time again. You'd need that dollop of info from Vienna or Sydney. You'd need somebody to run the damn Xerox machine at 1:00 a.m.

## The project life is not the "halfway" life.

And that's really it. For those who toil at EDS or Young & Rubicam, there's usually a Worthy Mission to accomplish. But "late" (as in a late proposal) isn't in the lexicon at EDS, any more than it is at the law firm whose associate misses the court's appellate filing deadline by a "mere" five minutes.

### T.T.D./Halfway = No Way

1. PSF chief: Talk loud and long and clear about the importance of pitching in as needed. Talk about triage. Talk about all-for-one-and-one-for-all. (Be as corny as you want.) **AND LIVE IT!** Make that 2:00 a.m. pizza run precisely because you are the boss; roll up your sleeves and get your hands dirty (changing the printer cartridge on the copy machine). Bottom line:

# Have you practiced
# Perceived Urgency today?
## ARE YOU SURE?

2. **Put "it"—mutual, unstinting support—in the formal evaluation process.** What gets measured, rewarded, and, yes, punished gets done or not done. ("I don't care how 'insanely great' Richard is. If he fails to support others in times of dire need … he's gone.")

3. **MBSA,** or Managing by Storying Around per Armstrong International's David Armstrong. (He wrote a book with that as its title. And it's his management philosophy.)

That is:

## Make Visible Heroes of the Insanely Busy People who sprinted the extra two miles to help another team.

How about an Extra Two Miles Hall of Fame? Or weekly/monthly Extra Two Miles Award?

# 22a.

Or: "One" is a beautiful word!

### *The Nub*

The seminar participant said that my "WOW! Projects stuff" made an enormous amount of sense. Her problem —in her nonprofit organization—was that she was stretched too thin, working on a half-dozen "important" projects at a time.

**"NO,"** I shouted. (More or less.) The project life is not the halfway life: See No. 22 above. And "total emotional commitment" to multiple projects … no matter how "important" each one … is simply impossible.

We all work on several things at a time, including Judy's seventh-grade science project that's due the day after tomorrow. (Same day as your client presentation.) Nonetheless, project-world *demands* singularity/serial monogamy … or something damn close to it.

Project performance excellence demands focus. No two ways about it. (I cannot compromise with you here. Been around too long.) Maybe there's some secondary stuff you're working on. (Sure, it *is* the real world.) Fine, but remember … it is *secondary*. Always … always …

**always** know what comes first and keep your eye/ heart/soul/mind firmly on the prize. Your "signature" project/legacy/life demands it.

## T.T.D./ Serial Monogamy

1. Assign full-time/totally obsessed souls to each project. They live/eat/breathe/sleep/love this project. They are *married* to this project—for better or for worse. Hone the project list until you have virtually everyone in your PSF married to a/one major project. Period.

# (Don't screw this up!)

2. Work this through with your Clients. Painstakingly. Make it clear that you'll produce guaranteed lousy results if you're spread too thin … no matter how "pressing" projects 3, 4, and 5 on the priority list are.

# 23.

Period.

*The Nub*

## It's so damn strange to me.

I can't remember the last time I visited an HR or Finance "Dept." with a Vision Statement.

## Why not?

Surely we—in accounting, HR, whatever—have aspirations of usefulness, of excellence, of cool. So why not state those aspirations … for one and all to see?

I guess the answer to "why not" is that such units have simply not seen themselves as independent actors. And that's one **(big)** thing this book aims to change.

Below you'll see the Values (Vision) Statement of a 25-person independent professional service firm. Read it at least once. Discuss it … with everyone. The group/PSF/Consulting-Training Firm that wrote it aspires to a global reputation. Cool people. Cool projects. Etc.

And you: You are the HR Department of the 600-person XYZ Division of Big Co.

**Don't you want that HR Dept. to be the-very-best-damn-HR-Dept.-in-the-whole-bloody-world at _s-o-m-e-t-h-i-n-g_?**

If not, W-H-Y N-O-T?

That's where I am on this. **PSF-Is-Cool. And we want to be recognized as Very-Damn-Special at what we do ... even if we are still a "Dept." in the division.**

And that means having a clear _vision_! It means standing for something ... striving for something ... struggling for something ... larger than ourselves. For something noble and uplifting and inspiring. (Forgive the hyperbole, but cynicism flat out frightens me. I want _you_ to have the best work life you can. I'm willing to go to the mat fighting for it. Are you?)

### ONE PROFESSIONAL SERVICE FIRM'S VALUES STATEMENT

1. _Do fabulous work and be known around the world for our innovativeness._

2. _Attract exciting people—more than a few of whom are a little offbeat._

3. _Raise Hell, constantly question "the way things are done around here," and never, ever rest on our laurels. (Today's laurels are tomorrow's compost.)_

**4.** *Make sure that those who leave us, voluntarily or involuntarily, can testify to having learned a lot, having had a special experience, and having made fast friends while they were here. (Ye shall be known by your alumni.)*

**5.** *Have a collegial, supportive, yeasty, zany, laughter-filled environment where people support one another, and politics is as absent as it can be in a human (i.e., imperfect) enterprise.*

**6.** *Insure that no question or innuendo ever arises about our ethics.*

**7.** *Dot the "i's," cross the "t's," answer the phones promptly, send out errorless invoices, and in general never forget that God is in the details.*

**8.** *Work with exciting customers (and other partners) who turn us on and stretch us, from whom we can learn, and with whom we enjoy associating. (And who pay their bills on time, too.) Fire dud customers.*

**9.** *Take in substantially more money than we spend. (Where spending includes above-average compensation and a very high level of investment in the future.)*

**10.** *Grow via creative, high-quality services and the acquisition of terrific clients—not via growth for growth's sake.*

Now that you've read the list, try this: Write down the negative of each statement. How's that sound!? (I.e.: Are you sure you don't want to sign up for these 10 attributes? Or some close kin?) Another trick: Score your unit on each item above. Score once on "desirability," once on "importance." Discuss!

## T.T.D./Getting with the Vision Thing!

**1.** Does your unit/dept. have a Vision Statement? If not, why not? (Discuss at length. It's important.) If you do, is it truly inspiring? Start by discussing vision statements in general ... the value thereof.

**2.** Collect a dozen Vision Statements from comparable Professional Service Firms.

**3.** Draft a prospective statement. (Keep it rough!) Talk through it—**for months!**—one word at a time. (Literally.)

**4.** Have everyone write a Personal Vision Statement: What does *he/she* stand for? In life? In work? Meld the personal statements with the unit aspirations. (*Hint:* They'd better line up pretty perfectly.)

**5. Challenge! Challenge! Challenge!** If we won't sign up for being "the best" ... *why not?*

# 23a.

A favorite discussion question when interviewing professional service providers, David Maister writes in *True Professionalism*, "is to ask people, 'Why do you do what you do?' Obviously things like money, meaning, and intellectual challenge are important, but the one I always listen for is **'I like helping people.'** If that one is missing, I know I am speaking with a professional in trouble."

TOM COMMENT: **Nice!**

### The Nub

"PSF-ing"—in accounting as well as human resources—is **a helping profession.** You're making people's lives easier ... you're alleviating their suffering (it may not be a gunshot wound, but it's certainly valid) ... you're solving problems ... bringing pleasure, convenience, ease, and excitement/WOW! into their lives. So if you don't get your jollies out of helping others, find something else to do. That's my advice.

I suggest that we take Mr. Maister very seriously and begin ... now ... to reframe our "practice" in account-

**ing, purchasing, whatever as a Helping Profession.**

Talk about it. What it means. (And doesn't.) Why it matters. Etc. I sincerely believe that such an ongoing dialogue could change your outlook, your perceptions, your self-esteem, and the performance of your "Dept."–turned-PSF.

### TWO EARS, ONE MOUTH

Okay! It's hackneyed! You know, the "Why did God give us two ears and one mouth?" bit. But it gets to the heart of the Helping Profession idea. In short, the professional services spawn a lot of experts—legitimate experts, no less—who blunt career effectiveness by falling in love with the sounds of their own voices.

I recently attended the retirement party for Jon Katzenbach, 40-year McKinsey & Co. consultant. He's undoubtedly one of the most effective folks the firm has produced. The consistency of the encomiums was noteworthy. (Downright spooky, actually.) "Katz," some noted, was probably not the keenest strategist McKinsey has ever spawned. But every one of his most senior colleagues went on and on … and then on some more … about his listening skills.

Reflecting on that, I realized I'd been around two other of McKinsey's all-time greats at moving Clients to action: my *In Search of Excellence* co-author, Bob Waterman, and former firm big cheese No. 1 Lee Walton. Both were smart as blazes, but what set them apart from their talented peers was understanding the 2:1 ear-to-mouth ratio. (Former star Harvard B. School prof Tony Athos reportedly told Walton he'd grant him a Ph.D. in clinical psychology anytime he wanted.)

Message: **To take "Helping Profession" idea from lip service to reality, calculate that ear-to-mouth ratio every morning!**

**T.T.D./**Helping Profession

1. **Hire people who like people!**

**Promote people who like people!**

Don't **hire people who don't like people!**

**God knows,** don't **promote people who don't like people!**

"The deepest principle in human nature," wrote psychologist William James, "is the craving to be appreciated." Great Client relationships—speaking practically—are an "appreciation business." Clients are not dunderheads because they are not as quick as you. They are real people, often very smart, who are wrestling with sticky, real-world, real-politics issues that cause them sometimes to pause where you pride yourself in "cutting to the chase"... no matter what the result in human damage.

2. TALK/TRAIN/OBSESS: HELPING PROFESSION. **Start by enumerating 15 (!) Attributes of a Helping PSF.** Make the ongoing dialogue around Helping Profession very transparent. (E.g.: Put the issue—explicitly—on every Weekly Operating Review agenda.) Have people you admire from the conventional "helping professions"—the head of nursing at the local hospital, etc.—address your colleagues. Run a special training program designed to sharpen "helping" skills. Encourage folks to volunteer one night a week teaching adults to read, helping the elderly, delivering hot meals to the homebound. Have them talk about the experience with their fellow PSFers.

# IV. live
# with 'em!

# 24.

Live with your Clients. (Love your Clients.)

## ENGAGE CLIENTS IN A
## VERY INTENSE/ I-N-T-I-M-A-T-E
## PROBLEM-SOLVING RITUAL/DANCE.

PSF-ing is a duet, not a solo performance. The idea is instinctive to some…anathema to others. But it's gotta be "gotten" by all! In short:

THE CLIENT MUST BE A SEAMLESS PART OF "IT" FROM START TO FINISH. AND BEYOND.

You want to deliver WOW! You want to make good on your promise of transformational change? Then get in bed with the Client. It's a pain at times: You know best. The Client hasn't got a clue. The Client has lousy bed-iquette. Is boorish and wildly demanding. Tough! Seduce/ Engage the Client. HE LIVES THERE—long after you're dust—AND YOU DON'T.

### *The Nub*

This may be the biggest difference between a "Dept." and a PSF. A PSF, no matter how proud…**sucks up**…to Clients.

PSF-ing is not a solo adventure. It's a shared journey. (E.g., read Tracy Kidder's *House*, about the architect-builder and Client minuet.)

It's not that Clients are smarter. (They may be or may not be.) It's that they pay your bills. And are your reason for existing!

"Living with" Clients—the best professional service firms' coda—means just that; as in "We are living with each other for the life of this project." It means they are...

## Full-Scale Members of Our Team.

(If the Client won't give you full-time, top-flight members, beg off the project. The Client isn't serious.) It means you spend most of your time—80 percent?—on the Client's premises. It means you commit yourself—intellectually *and* emotionally *and* physically—to a Genuine Joint Venture. A marriage.

## "WE"-ISM

I did "it" just this morning. Gave a speech. Prior to my bit, a singer had performed. She was very good. I was with a Client exec. I said, instinctively, "Is she one of **ours**... or an outsider?" "Outsider," was the Client's immediate response. This was a two-hour gig on my part. But my decades-old McKinsey & Co. indoctrination shone through: *For those two precious hours, I was totally insinuated into the Client's Identity. I was Married to that Client ... body/mind/soul. We were ... well ... WE.*

Sure, it "pays." Me. But it's also the way I feel!

# I LIVE FOR THEM ("US") ... AS I DO THAT GIG. PERIOD. IT IS NOT PHONY. (AND I'LL FIGHT YOU TO THE BITTER END IF YOU SUGGEST IT IS.)

## T.T.D./Client Intimacy/Co-identity!

**1.** In project "negotiations" ... insist that the Client give you top-tier talent as full-time team partners. Even if you are (still) a "Dept.," walk away from the project if this demand is not met.(Seriously.) If they try to pawn off second-rank folks on you or offer the better people only part-time, they just aren't making the commitment that a Successful Marriage demands.

**2.** Set up a **PSF-Client Review Board,** pretty darn formally, to jointly track project progress. It's a good way to nip potential problems in the bud. Remember: The key to any successful marriage is communication ... communication ... communication.

**3.** Make sure that your team members are (mostly) living at the Client's. **(Period.)**

**4.** As PSF boss, set up a routine (weekly?) "Check in" call with your Client counterpart. **(Period.)**

**5.** Consider drafting a simple yet compelling Joint Venture Aims "document" to guide the evolving project's progress.

# 24a.

Literally: Live with 'em.

### The Nub

Bill Caudill and friends took a lot of heat from their professional peers. But they ended up reinventing the practice of architecture. Caudill, founder of Caudill, Rowlett, Scott (now CRS Sirrine), and Wally Scott were working on their first school, in Blackwell, Oklahoma, in 1948. They submitted their plan. The Client rejected it. Then did so again. And a third and fourth time as well. Money was very tight. What to do?

The answer: "squat." That is, Caudill said to Scott, "Wally, we're going to lose our shirts if we don't do something quick. How about you and me loading the drafting boards in your car [Caudill's car was so old it wouldn't have stood the 525-mile trip], driving to Blackwell, and squatting, like Steinbeck's Okies, in the boardroom until we get the damn plans approved?" Squat is what Caudill and Scott did. The architects were thought odd at first, but curiosity got the better of the local school board members, who started dropping by and offering their two cents' worth of advice. Soon enough, the plan was accepted unanimously.

Over the subsequent fifty years, "squatters" at CRS Sirrine became the cornerstone for creating some of the world's most complex structures. The process was refined to a high art ... down to size and paper-stock specifications for the little white "snow cards," used to record and display ideas during intense, marathon joint planning sessions.

The architectural establishment was initially appalled to see Virtuoso Performance "compromised" by such heavy-handed Client-kibitzing. But Caudill moved from triumph to triumph ... and his ideas have now found significant, if not universal, acceptance.

Moral (lesson ... for you and me):

## Living with the Client—when it truly means "living with"—can pay enormous dividends.

And, still, far too few professional service firms, let alone depts., pay homage to this rigorous discipline.

### T.T.D./Squat!

1. So: **Squat!** That is, for starters, most Client project work should be done from scrounged and spartan offices on the Client premises. Flip normal logic: There must be a damn good reason for you and yours *not* to be "at the Client's."

2. Steal from CRS Sirrine: **Develop a methodology for intense, joint problem-solving with**

**the Client.** (See, in *Liberation Management*, my extensive write-up of "the method" at CRS Sirrine.)

3. Take this damn seriously!

# 24b.

Openly, purposefully share your knowledge and wisdom. The goal is clear (or, at least, it ought to be):

## We want the Client to stay turned on—autonomously—to "our stuff" when we exit, stage right.

So, transferring knowledge/excitement/wisdom/WOW! is all-important. Thence our commitment is not to "hoarding stuff" but to sharing it freely and openly, including our "proprietary" methodology for approaching/framing problems. (THIS IS A BIG DEAL.)

P.S. I repeat: There is no genuine/lasting knowledge transfer without first-rate Client Team Members. Moreover, the Client Team Members must be treated as "real players." There is sometimes a tendency on the part of PSF "experts" to look down their noses at the unwashed. Forget it! (**And punish it** ... if it comes to your attention!)

## *The Nub*

A few years ago McKinsey & Co. shifted its Practice. All problem-solving would now be done with Client teams as Full Partners. My *In Search of Excellence* co-author, Bob Waterman, built a high-impact consulting practice on the bedrock of Client-Partnering-in-Problem-Solving: The Client took away the tested McKinsey-Waterman Approach to problem analysis, as much as the solution to a particular problem.

Such an approach—**giving away your Core Methodology**—is rare. But it shouldn't be. If I'm in HR working on some new Web-centric ideas about hiring with one of our divisions, my unabashed goal—as I see it —is to get my Client turned on about the payoff from effective hiring. I want the Client to be passionate about and competent in, say, Web-centric hiring when I leave the scene. That is: I want to transfer the know-how, the passion, and the technology! I want to create autonomous Fanatics who will carry the **(IMPORTANT.** I hope.) torch when I've exited.

Alas, this philosophy flies in the face of a lot of conventional practice, which says, in effect, "Hold tight to your special knowledge at all costs." I find that to be a morally bankrupt approach. My job, as a professional, is to grow daily. (And dramatically, over time.) Hence I do the best I can today to give away today's "secrets." My only strategic defense-offense, then, is to struggle mightily to stay ahead of the power curve.

## T.T.D./Obsessive "Technology" Transfer!

1. Are the Client Members on our project team just providing information? Or are they working through and grasping our Core Methodology for approaching problems?

   **(1a.** Redux: See No. 24 above. No project without top-flight client-partners on the team. **Full-time.** Period!)

2. Make a point of working on the Client premises. But/and also make a point of having the Client hanging out at our place.

3. After the project, consider having a Client Team Member work on another project with us … to cement her mastery of our approach.

# 24c.

## ENGAGE CLIENTS IN A MEASURED "RISK PROGRESSION" PROCESS.

You want the client to "go for the gold." Right? Fine. But there is a crystal-clear correlate: If you want the Client to stick his/her/its neck out … tomorrow … then you damn well better have fully engaged him/her in "the process" from the start.

That is, true "risk taking" is a Joint Venture/Journey. We get to know each other—to *trust* each other—and then (and only then!) can we consider leaping off a Cliff-Called-WOW! together.

## We are in the Joint Venture Business. Period.

### *The Nub*

It is clear. (Or it should be.) We want WOW! Which means we want the Client to bungee-jump with us. Guess what: Far easier said than done.

Problem No. 1 with most projects out of IS, HR, whatever: The Client balks at the change menu being proposed. It's too much (too radical/too freaky) too soon.

Answer: There is only one.

## We and the Client must engage in an adventure that is based on mutual trust and understanding.

And since we—WOW!-ing PSFers that we are—are leading the journey, we must take the Clients by the hand (especially at first) and walk them through the pre-jump jitters. We must prove that we are knowledgeable, skilled, passionate guides looking out for their welfare. Then when we reach the cliff's edge, they will be ready to take the leap of faith.

In its heyday, Chiat/Day took some pretty stuffy clients to the brink. Their secret: Turn normal ad agency practice on its head. Chiat/Day didn't "hide the creatives" from the clients until the 23rd hour, then spring a "cool" surprise. They got the client *and* the creatives together on Day No. 1, and the two trained together as they moved out of the comfort zone ... farther ... and then farther still.

I guess this is one more, albeit nuanced, plea for true joint venturing. If you want the Client to go where None Have Dared Go Before, then we need to lay the groundwork...**together**.

I don't much know what to do other than exhort:

# We fail!—as PSFers— if we can't get the Client to Take the Plunge.

(With us.) Thence little is of higher priority than emotionally-engaging-the-Client-in-our-Bold-Quest-from-the-First-Step. Right?

### T.T.D./Bungee-Jumping Duos!

1. **Introduce the idea of a Bold Quest** ... and Adventure...at the top of the process, during initial project formulation and negotiation. (Consider using those words or ones that are equally "hot.") Talk about the Parameters of an Adventure ... of Mutual Exploration ... of the Joint Legacy of WOW We Hope to Create.

2. Tolerate "fuzzy." Don't try to suggest that you have the answer. Make clear—**is it to you?**—that there is no foreordained answer, that we really do plan to Explore

New Pastures Together. (PSF chief: Make sure your staff buys into this! If they play "the wise ones," it'll backfire! Adventures into the Unknown are about both of us taking the plunge ... mutually risking our professional reputations.)

**3.** Though fuzzy about the path, be clear about **The Methodology**. (See No. 33 below): We may not know where we'll end up, but we do have a (proven) process for proceeding on our journey. And also be clear about the passion. Assure the Client that it's true, firm, and will not fade when the going gets tough (as it will).

# 25.

When the time comes for promotion decisions, de-brief Key Clients on the long-term performance of the employee(s) under consideration. Also, ask the Clients to evaluate the quality of their own employees' work on joint projects; this adds a hearty dose of reality to membership on the project team (and keeps the assignment from being some sort of "sabbatical").

### The Nub

**Salesmen know.** They are always evaluated by their Clients: They make the sale … or they don't.

Makes sense to me … and for me … and all of us. You invite me to speak to your group. Thanks.

## But do you invite me back?

I want to be independent, feisty, provocative … *and* I want to be invited back!

All of this is a slightly long-winded way of encouraging you—Ms. PSF—to have Clients formally evaluate your team members (and you!) during, after, and long after a project. What holds for salespeople and for Tom-Peters-the-speaker should hold for Mary-Jenkins-the-accountant working on a systems project for an internal Client in the Purchasing Department.

(It would also be terrific if you could talk your PSF-peer in the Purchasing Dept./Purchasing Inc. into letting you evaluate his project team members' performance. After all, doing cool, joint-venture projects will be *the* name of *the* game ... for *all* of us. And what's good for the goose ...)

## T.T.D./Client-led Evaluations

1. As part of the project's formal scope, set up a structure for the Client to formally evaluate your team members. (And vice versa, if you are so inclined.) Make this a part of the initial project negotiation.

2. Develop with the Client—*and* the team members —the framework and parameters of the evaluation. Discuss it openly! (And at length.) This isn't some kind of secret assessment. One and all should know that they will be evaluated ... and they should know by what measures.

3. Use Client evaluations of project managers, a year or so after the project is complete, as the centerpiece for promotion decisions. (E.g.: Did Bob Smith's project "stick" ... have lasting impact?)

# 25a.

## Think independent.

### *The Nub*

In *True Professionalism*, author and PSF guru David Maister tells this story on himself:

> I will never forget the best piece of career advice I ever received. I was a young assistant professor at the Harvard Business School, eager to figure out what I had to do to get tenure (i.e., "make partner"). I went to one of the elder statesmen of the school to find out what was required of me.
>
> "You're asking the wrong question, David," he said. "The rule here is very simple. If the rest of the world wants you, we'll probably want you. If the rest of the world doesn't want you, we probably won't want you. Focus on being the best you can be at what you want to do."

The idea I take from this: My job—as PSF boss—is to make sure that every person who works for me sees herself or himself as an Independent Actor whose performance in the end will be judged—almost solely—by the Outside World.

That is, she or he is charged with delivering the goods, making a difference ... for the Client ... period.

Maister then quotes the lawyer Fred Bartlit on the reasons why "professional life" should be "the most exciting career there is":

> *Professionals are interesting, smart people who are interesting to spend time with. The problems we face are fascinating and are different almost every day. We learn about many different businesses. We deal with many different clients. We are not stuck in a rut of having the same boss for ten years. Because we deal with ideas, one person can make a difference. We deal with cutting-edge issues. As professionals, we do not have "bosses." We work for ourselves and have only ourselves to satisfy. We have a lot of personal freedom. We do not have to be in a particular place every day at a particular time.... The [professions], then, should be a terrific way to spend time. We work in small groups of highly motivated, interesting people, addressing ever-changing, complex problems where there is a lot at stake. What could be better?*

## Big words. Big meaning.

But that's the whole point. And it's the wonderful/ennobling/liberating message of "PSF-ing" at its best!

## T.T.D./The World at Large Shall Judge You and Your Aspirations!

1. PSF boss: Make it clear to your colleagues—from your body language to your formal policies—that judgment lies in the external world. The Client's world. The World of Demonstrated Performance. The World of the Work Itself.

2. Discuss the specific words above. Do they have meaning/relevance to you? Your gang? Perhaps work with an outside facilitator on the personal/professional relevance of the above. Is it "too much"? If so ... why? If it reverberates close to your collective souls, what do we do next?

# 26.

Period. **But** don't lose your independent voice. Think
Client. **And**: Stay autonomous. Keep working on what
makes you fabulous and unique irrespective of the
Client. Think … impact!

## Cherish the great tension!

### The Nub

I learned it on Hour No. 1 at McKinsey & Co. You live for
your Client! Then on about Hour No. 3 I met my great
mentor, partner Allen Puckett. And he taught me: *Push
the Client past his or her comfort zone in your unrelent-
ing quest for lasting impact. Never the twain shall meet.*
Exactly. (At least.)

Client-centric? **Amen!** I crawl on my knees to that
altar to this day. (I do occasionally—literally—get down
on my knees before a Client.) But my other altar is provocative work. And there **is** a conflict between the two.
If you're so damn provocative that nothing gets implemented … well … then … you're just egocentric. **(And
sometimes that is warranted.)** On the other
hand, if you're so bloody Client-centric (i.e., focused on
signing up the next job with said Client) that you sacri-
fice your independence and play it safe—and I've seen

this a hundred times—then you're a **Charlatan** in my book. (And this *is* my book.)

## T.T.D./Acknowledging the Irreducible Tension!

**1.** PSF boss: *Every* week. *Every* project. Ask the same question: What's the l-e-g-a-c-y? Is this WOW!? Will it make a difference? Does it provoke? Is it worth doing?

And: *Every* week. *Every* project. Are we listening to the Client? Engaging the Client? Co-inventing with the Client? Transferring knowledge and enthusiasm to the Client?

Consciously drive down both these roads. **Fast.**

**2.** Talk up the Great Tension with your PSF colleagues. This is the heart of the superior Professional Service Firm. Please: Do not brush this issue under the rug.

**3. Put both "sides" of this tension-paradox into the formal personal evaluation criteria and equation.**

**4. Talk about this tension—starting during the negotiation process—with the Client herself.**

Continue to talk with the Client about this issue as the Engagement proceeds. Make it clear: You want her to be your full-fledged partner. *And*: You want her and you to be scrapping to define, finally, a rockin' project you'll both be bragging about…**10** years from now.

# 27.

Consultants need consultants!

Sounds like a bad joke. It's not.

All the best PSF folk I've worked with have stupendous "personal universities," as one called it. That is, they've consciously nurtured a stable of cool/far-out contacts who keep them fertile. They routinely add to that stable … and then use the services of their on-the-leading-edge buddies to push their project work to the edge. And beyond.

*It is the worst sort of conceit—especially these wacky days—to imagine you've got all the resources/knowledge/know-how you need at home.*

### The Nub

## All experts need experts!

Again, this insight emanates from my McKinsey & Co. mentor Allen Puckett. Allen enhanced every project we worked on with strange ducks from hither and thither: Harvey Wagner, decision-sciences guru and professor;

David Montgomery, quantitative marketing genius and professor; Gerald Hillman, iconoclast economist.

Allen is perhaps the smartest guy I've ever met. And …clearly…**the most curious.** He was determined to expand the perspective—dramatically—of any assignment he encountered. And we did so by counseling with his Rolodex of Freaks. (My term … not his. Though he would approve.)

Not only have I tried to follow modestly in his footsteps, but I have observed that this is a common trait among the best of breed in *any* professional service firm (or *any* profession at all, for that matter). The best are bound and determined to bring a quirky/surprising/state-of-the-art perspective to all of their work. And the only way to do that (I am convinced) is to "collect" freaks! And then use them!

To which you say, "I'm not a partner at McKinsey & Co. with access to the world." To which I say: Rubbish!

You go to a restaurant this Saturday evening. First time. The service is scintillating. On Monday (or right then and there), you call the restaurateur and ask her if *you* can take *her* to lunch … and drain her brain. You do just that. You add her to your Rolodex. And when you are next working on a service issue, you call her (or pay her a consulting fee, for a couple of days) to work with you, your team, and your Client.

## Okay?

That's a way a Collector of Cool Dudes-Dudettes-Freaks starts! Mindset and determination are far more important than position in the pecking order.

### T.T.D./Freaks-on-Call!

**1.** You're at work on a project. Perhaps stuck in at least a little rut. Rack your brain:

## Whom have you met at a conference in the last year who might have a quirky-different perspective to bring to bear?

Take the plunge. Seize the moment. Call her/him ... and ask if you can chat ... or e-chat ... about your conundrum.

**2.** You are off to an HR/IS/Whatever conference in two weeks. You go to a small breakout session. The presenter has a really intriguing point of view. At least ask for her/his e-mail address. At best, ask if you can buy her/him a drink tonight.

## Never—ever!—let a conference pass without adding a **half-dozen** (some would say 25! no kidding!) freaks to your Cool Dudes-Dudettes Rolodex.

**3.** Now apply this idea to your day-to-day experience: e.g., at that cool restaurant.

**4.** Religiously "use" these ("cool") people on all of your projects. (And, of course, stand by to be used by them. Reciprocity rules!)

# V. a culture of urgency!

# 28.

The Client challenges us. We have crafted a WOW! Project in response. Fine! But it ain't enough. That is, the best of the PSFs work hard and consciously to create a vibrant environment. These stellar performers know that energy and excitement beget more of same. They know that people simply function at higher levels when they're in a vital setting.

## The Nub

IDEO Design & Product Development in Palo Alto is frenetic ... resembling nothing so much as a gaggle of kindergarten classrooms. Moreover, IDEO thinks nothing of having everyone stop work on a second's notice ... to join in a "brainstormer" ... during which all hands gather around for a lightning-fast session—with Clients—to chew on a problem.

Fact is, I've visited hundreds of companies over the last 20 years. But I've been in only four places where I said, "Hey, I could work here." They were: **IDEO**; **Imagination**, the British marketing services firm; **CNN**; and **Bloomberg**, the financial information-services company.

All four are PSFs. All four thrive/live/die on WOW Projects. And all four vibrate with excitement. **They "rock."**

## And: They rock ... by conscious design.

All four are homes to an inordinate share of young/youngish people on the make. (In the best sense of that word.) All four let the newest recruit know that

## "It's up to you to carve your own path."

All four make it clear that "there are no 'rules' which get in the way of fantastic-quirky performance." All four make it clear that they are in a hurry to get (Very Cool) things done.

Is all this easy to achieve in your newly liberated "Purchasing Inc."? No. **(Hell, no.)** Is it worth the effort to try? "Absolutely," is my unstinting reply. Even if you don't reach the levels of the superstars above, you'll be better for the trying; and in this case half/quarter a loaf is far better than none at all.

Great PSFs—I love 'em!—are Cool Places.

**(This book is dedicated to creating** Cool Places ... where your only limits are your imagination and energy ... **and to de-Dilbertizing the white collar workplace.)**

How do you pull off the CNN-IDEO-Imagination-Bloomberg magic? It is unimaginably difficult. Still ...

Here are a few ideas:

**1.** First, as PSF boss, you've got to convince *yourself* that this (HR, Finance, etc.) is a **Rockin' Adventure**, worthy of extreme emotional commitments by you and your colleagues.

**2.** You've got to WOW!-the-Bloody-Hell out of every project and turn it into an Adventure-Quest.

**3.** You've got to "cool up" the joint ... make it actually **vibrate with excitement**. (Which starts with you ... personally ... Ms./Mr. PSF.) This means paying attention to design, color, layout, furniture, etc. It means setting new policies that both symbolically and literally loosen things up ... things like the "instant brainstormers" at IDEO ... or casual *every*days ... or field trips to other PSFs to gain inspiration and "borrow" ideas on creating a happenin' environment.

*You've been to phat places ... right? Restaurants? Theater performances? Conferences? What—very specifically—makes them phat? A phat restaurant and phat HR Dept. are one and the same ... as I see it. Think about it.*

### PHAT PSFs: A.K.A. HOT GROUPS!

When I search for reading material on this topic—"cool" PSFs—I don't find much. And that's an understatement. But recently off the press is a marvelous exception. It's a book called *Hot Groups* by professor-futurists Jean Lipman-Blumen and Hal Leavitt. The wildly gyrating nature of the world, they insist, means that more and more work will be done by energetic teams brought together for short periods of time. The main attributes of those teams: They ...

* Are task-obsessed!

* Are passionate!

* Ennoble the Work Itself.

* Are the *opposite* of "self-managed teams" and "task forces" (they are created to do "hot work" ... not to perform ordinary service in a teamlike way).

* Are of short/shortish duration.

* Think like children (brilliantly naïve).

* Make enemies (all determined change agents do).

* Are obsessive, sometimes secretive, cherish the role of underdog.

* Cut and try (live by what I call Quick Prototyping Mania).

* Recruit cool people!

* Believe "sell" is not a dirty word! (Life in the projects is ... sales. Just as it is in community-organizing.)

* Are youthful. Encourage individuals to "be themselves."

* Grow in loose, rich organizational soil.

* Can become the cornerstone of an overall organizational strategy if the top leaders act as "seeders, feeders, and weeders" of such groups.

Lipman-Blumen and Leavitt's "hot groups" are about as close to my **Hot-Cool-Phat PSF** as you can get. Hooray! I have good company here!

## T.T.D./Cool!

1. Step 1: Think about this! Take it seriously! Talk with two or three of your colleagues: What would a "Cool HR Dept." look like? Feel like? Smell like? Write down 10 **(or better yet . . . no kidding . . . 50)** Characteristics of **HR Inc.-as-Rockin' Joint**. Consider a "game plan" for the 10 most important of those 50 characteristics.

2. Step 2 is to step back. What would make us "really proud of this place"? List 10—no more, **and no less**— Characteristics of a Seminal IS Department. (IS Inc.!) Spend a lot of time on this.

3. Visit some "cool" professional service firms (the area's hottest ad agency or software house, for example). Talk to the leaders. Ask the leaders to come in and talk to your gang.

4. WOW PSFers do WOW Work for WOW Clients. Talk to your Clients about this.

Ask the Client:

**What would we "look like" if we were Cool-Beyond-Measure?** How do we **"cool up"** the current project? Perhaps repeat with the Client the formal, make-the-list-of-characteristics exercise above.

# Great PSFs Give Great Theater!

# 29.

I love the term "studio" for all it conjures up: a place ...most likely a highly idiosyncratic place ...dedicated to a specific creative endeavor. I urge you to reconfigure your Dept.'s work space as a design studio.(You know, the design and execution of WOW! Projects.)

Project teams should all have homes—hangouts— where they can nest and work. Space is usually at a premium, but such nests should be big enough to include Client members. And they should be designed/configured/created by the team members themselves (this alone is a great identity-building exercise).

### The Nub

I *do* love the term ... **"studio."** It brings to mind Picasso, Pavarotti, Frank Lloyd Wright, the great industrial designer Henry Dreyfuss. A studio is a setting where "seriously cool" work gets done. A studio isn't just a room; it is a "charged" place that aids and abets the work, that stimulates and inspires the creator(s), that provides a safe haven where the muses can flourish.(And wounds can be licked.) The studio is in fact a full-fledged partner in the PSF process! **My own take: Space matters! A lot!** (A lot more than most of us think.)

If we want to produce Rockin' Stuff, we need a Rockin' Space. Fact: Most bosses, even PSF bosses, pay far too little attention to space. If a "place" vibrates, then the odds go up—dramatically!—that you and I who inhabit it will "vibrate" as well.

So: I beg you to "think about" space. If "it" is dull and dreary, so, too, will be the projects produced therein. If "it" is Hot-Cool-Phat ... well ... the odds do go (way) up that the projects produced therein will be ... Hot-Cool-Phat.

## T.T.D./"Hot Spaces"

1. So, what do you think? Can Space = Spunk? Ponder it. Talk about it. Do something about it.

2. Take a hard look at your work space. (Right now.) Does it exude "good (hot!) vibes"? Or not?

3. Benchmark "rockin' places." Restaurants. Theaters. Architects' work spaces. Buy some books. Start reading ... studying. Invite some experts in. Become a student of Hot Places. This stuff matters: IT'S WORTH STUDYING.

4. What can you *do* ... **in the next 48 hours** ... to launch a Space Matters Initiative? Meet with your gang: "How can we 'hot up' the workplace/space to reflect our 'hot' aspirations?" (Create a list of at least **25** items.)

# 30.

PSF work is an all-out affair. So bumping up morale is a constant concern. (Sure, things are exciting … but also emotional and exhausting.) One of the better morale-boosting "tools": religiously throwing little, spontaneous celebrations to honor a milestone passed, a proposal submitted, a contract won.

### The Nub

"PSF-World" is all about … **emotion.**

## We care! The work (project) matters! We invest a whole helluva lot of our-selves—physically, emotionally, intel-lectually, spiritually!

If "all that" is true, then we experience downs (many) and ups (many … we hope). And (human as we are) we need/thrive on regular reminders that what we are doing is appreciated and important. Celebrations are also wonderful arenas for bonding; they bring folks to-gether … add levity … and spontaneity … and spark.

My (bigger) point: We need to seriously consider the peaks and valleys that are the natural rhythm of PSF work. We need to pump up those who are strung out...hit with an unexpectedly early deadline...or the failure of a prototype. We need to find excuses—the smallest success—to celebrate and cheer.

You are demanding! (Fine.) (These are demanding times; that's the point of this series of books.) But make celebration—and joy!—as much a mainstay of your leadership routine as criticism.

## Work on it. Consciously. All the time.

### T.T.D./Celebrate!

1. The gang is under continual pressure. It's the best reason to find **s-o-m-e-t-h-i-n-g** to celebrate. **Now.** The idea: We want our PSF to be a "Rockin' Place." Right? Which means handing out regular kudos to those who exhibit great energy...and passion...for what they do. So, how's your "Kudos Scorecard"?

2. Simple point: **Celebrate. Cool stuff. (Including "small" Cool stuff.) Regularly. Period.**

3. As in: **When was the last time you threw a tiny, spontaneous celebration?** (If the answer is "More than 48 hours ago"...subtract points.)

**When was the last time you stopped by someone's workstation to say thanks**

—in person—for a small-but-special effort? (If the answer is "More than 24 hours ago"... subtract points.)

**When was the last time you sent a generic "Way to Go" e-mail to the team?**

When was the last time you sent a "Way to Go" e-mail to a *Client* team member? To a subcontractor who delivered with flair?

**When was the last time that you brought in a big bunch of tulips ... "just" to perk up the place?**

Do you in fact have a literal, formal notebook (electronic or paper), in which you keep more-than-casual track of the kudos you've delivered? (Think of it as a **THANK YOU Reminder Pad.**)

The point: Think about this stuff. Constantly. More or less formally. Then act. Constantly.

# 30a.

There are bad days at the office.

## Dealing with the emotional roller coaster called PSF-on-a-Holy-Mission takes thoughtful effort!

### *The Nub*

Life stinks ... upon (regular?) occasion. That is: If you attempt WOW! ... you will get your nose bloodied. Frequently. It's part of the game. The price of admission.

Which, therefore, means: A lot of the PSF boss's job is helping the troops grin-and-bear-it in the face of "unfair" setbacks.

It's ironic, I suppose, that having the nerve to stretch, to step out (far) from the norm means that we will suffer inordinate pain ... as well as (perhaps) Ultimate Glory. In any event, it makes the PSF boss' job more one of managing the emotional downs—and ups—than of being a glorified chief scheduler. For which all honchos should be externally grateful. I mean ... what's more rewarding: picking nits ... or helping soften the bumps along the road to personal/professional fulfillment for a bunch of wonderful/cool/dedicated folks?

While I am always leery of overusing sports analogues (it's such a cheap Guy Thing), this topic certainly lends itself to those well-worn metaphors. Consider a 16-game, regular National Football League season. The coaching staff's job is at least as much managing the emotional superhighs—and superlows!—as it is getting the X's and O's on the chalkboard right. A loss—on, say, *Monday Night Football*, in front of 30 million viewers—is followed by a shortened week of preparation before the next game ... a full one-sixteenth of the season ... in which the team is trying to (1) recover from the humiliation of losing in front of half the nation, (2) deal with disappointed fans, friends, and family, (3) suffer the slings and arrows of the often hostile and mocking media, and (4) prepare for the next game. Talk about emotional/physical/spiritual/intellectual overload! Whoa! And winning, believe it or not, is no day at the beach; it carries its own set of expectations, pressures, letdowns. In any event, the point: The **conscious management-of-emotion** is a big part of the leader's job.

So, too, in "PSF-in-Pursuit-of-WOW-world."

### T.T.D./Conscious Momentum Management

## 1. Get clear with yourself: If you are "on a mission," there will be bad days.

So make it plain to the team that it's normal ... even good ... if they're feeling less than fabulous at certain times. (In fact, there are few things more annoying, wearying, or suspect than someone who is perpetually "up." 'Tain't natural.) Downs = Okay. (As well, of course, as ups!) That's what "chasing important stuff" is all about!

2. No matter how grand your cause, there are "doldrums." A bad-week-at-the-office doesn't mean that life as we know it has ended. So, no baloney, "enjoy" the doldrums as well as the good times. It's part of life ... **if** ... you are up to something worthwhile. Be sensitive to those with the blues; be gentle ... give them space to work it through (this is not the same as condoning self-indulgent moaning/whining).

### 3. Keep the emotions and emotionality out on the table.

Don't hide it! Don't treat it as unnatural! ("Taking the emotion out of business" is exactly where B. Schools have gone so dreadfully wrong.) Talk about emotion and project roller coasters. Bring in the occasional outside coach or facilitator. (Maybe have a local clinical psychologist give a Brown Bag Lunch address sometime.) I'm hardly suggesting that we "psychologize ourselves to death." I am suggesting that we deal openly with the emotional turmoil associated with Worthy Quests. Denying emotion is a *sure* prescription for disaster because it *will* come out one way or another. (We've all been in offices that seethe with barely repressed resentments. Ugly places. Real WOW killers.) Hence, your best bet as boss is to understand and, to the extent possible, take control of the emotional climate.

## 4. Take breaks!

There's little that's more important! (Truly.) A 15-minute time out, for a trot or walk around the block, is worth its weight in gold. As PSF chief: When was the last time, at two o'clock in the afternoon, that you went up to a stressed team member and said, "Get Out of Here... for half an hour... and go to Starbucks"? When was the last time you went up to a stressed-out soul and said, "Take tomorrow off. I know it'll drive you crazy. Do it anyway. It's an order"?

## 5. Toy Time!

There are few better stress relievers than toys and games. (Why do you think so many Silicon Valley companies have invested in basketball courts, Ping-Pong tables, pool tables, and swimming pools? S'not altruism.) So ... invest in a toy chest! Appoint a Mistress of Fun and Games.

6. PSF boss:

# YOUR JOB ...
# MANAGER OF EMOTIONAL RHYTHM!

(Don't forget that.)

# 30b.

### *The Nub*

Yo Lily Tomlin! Yo John Cleese! Yo Court Jester!

(And I'm not kidding!)

I've been on a dozen "cool" project teams. If they *are* cool…you are under constant tension.(Life ain't fair: No good deed—rockin' project—goes unpunished!)

Which means you need an antidote:

# BRING IN THE CLOWN(S)!

Bottom line: You need—desperately—someone(s) with a fabulous sense of humor to liven things up and to break the tension that comes along, as inevitable baggage, with a Worthwhile Quest.

### T.T.D./Bring in the Clown(s)!

1. **We need comic relief.** We need to make sure we don't take ourselves too seriously.(Since…in fact… we *are* up to "big"-cool-very-serious stuff.) Consider this. Talk about it with your colleagues.

**2.** To make "cool stuff happen" is ... an **art form**. An art form that requires us to consciously cultivate a sense of play and playfulness. Thence: Look for specific opportunities to inject levity into the proceedings:

* Proffer corny awards. Regularly.

* Call play breaks. Literally.

* Schedule trips to the park. Have review meetings in the park.

* Have costume day. "Dress-up" day. "Dress-down" day.

* Figure out who on your crew has the best sense of humor. Urge/encourage her to make use of it. (Appoint her **Mistress of Larks and Levity**?) Ridiculous notices ... computer-created composites of Joe with Tom Cruise's bod ... or maybe with Pamela Anderson's. Whatever gets folks chuckling is okay.

**3. Recruit team members—at least some —with an eye on sense of humor.** This is an Arctic Voyage we are undertaking. And the nights can be long (very) and cold (very). Think the way Captain Scott and Admiral Peary would have thought about team member selection as they headed off on their epic experiences of discovery. *(That's what you're up to, right?)*

# 31.

## (It's an order!)

All PSFs have support staff—junior researchers, reports experts, IS geeks, etc. Alas, these folks are usually treated as second-class citizens, who rank miles beneath the lawyers, designers, programmers, architects. Mistake!

Great PSF-ing is a Team Sport. Wise PSF chiefs pay particularly close attention to the love, care, and feeding (and rewarding!) of the Unsung Heroes of PSF-World.

### The Nub

There was a clear—all too clear!—pecking order at McKinsey & Co., as there is at every law firm, ad agency, etc. To be sure, this is somewhat natural and part of the beast: The star litigator, architect, rainmaking partner is just that ... a star.

On the other hand, PSF-ing, like baseball and opera, calls for lots more than home run hitters and golden-throated divas. In particular, there is an all-important support staff that does the research grunt work ...

maintains the databases ... prepares the reports to the clients ... and so on.

In the one-person accountancy, "the woman" is dependent—utterly!—on the part- or full-time office administrator, even in this age of Microsoft Office, pagers, and cell phones.

*Messages:*

* Recruit and hire support staff with care and the same exacting standards you apply to hiring the young lawyers or accountants.

* Compensate the support staff well.

* Be particularly mindful of including the support staff in kudos given and other "soft" rewards.

* **Treat the support staff with the respect they deserve.**
  (Kudos and even money will soon lose their luster if folks are being treated like second-class citizens.)

In my experience, the most successful young PSF "line" professionals were those wise enough to cozy up to the support staff; they would be rewarded with a level of service and commitment to die for.

(To this day, more than 20 years later, I probably have more support staff pals than consultant pals from my seven years at McKinsey & Co.)

## T.T.D./Create Support Staff Heroes!

**1.** Carefully think through the structure of the PSF's support staff. Even if you are (very) resource-strapped, err toward more, not less.

**2.** Recruit support staff with care! For the tiny PSF, most support staff will be sub-contractors: Choose contractors who are small and on the move ... who will partner with you and take you seriously.

**3.** Don't be chintzy! (On the other hand, don't make the mistake of thinking that the most expensive contractor is the best. Again: The vigorous, imaginative, on-the-make contractor may give you much more care and attention than the "famous" provider of services. You want someone whose hunger and passion match your own.)

**4.** As a matter of rigorous habit, make sure that the support staff shares fully in the *emotional* rewards of the WOW! Project Life. Think about this consciously. **Daily!** Do something about it. Consciously. **Daily!**

# 32.

Project(s) Life = Deadline(s) Life.

Each project—in the unit as a whole/the PSF—needs a "deadlines/scheduling/milestones freak." Sounds like administrivia. It ain't!

"How does the project get to be a year and a half behind schedule? One day at a time!"—the word according to Fred Brooks, fabled IBM System 360 project manager, writing in *The Mythical Man-Month*.

## That is,
## the Keeper of the Master Schedule
## has another name in the PSF:
## God.

### The Nub

PSF-ing is Cool! PSF-ing is WOW! That's been the main thrust of this book, and indeed of this series of books (and indeed of my life).

Nonetheless: **Hats (w-a-y) off to the anal-retentive Milestone Freak!** (Please excuse the strong language. I think it's warranted.)

Discipline and WOW!-Cool **are** handmaidens. Not archenemies. In fact, they are 100 percent co-dependent. As Warren Bennis and Patricia Ward Biederman say in their fantastic book *Organizing Genius,* "Great groups ship." I.e.: It ain't great (Cool, WOW!) till it's done! And it's not gonna get done without someone being vigilant (obsessive!) about deadlines, milestones, files, and budgets.

Whether it's a support staff member or the Managing Partner herself is a matter of indifference. The idea:

# Someone—respected!—has to be the Deadline Dragon.

Projects—far more than rote tasks—are *all* surprise-laden. Unless it's ambiguous, it's rarely worth doing. Nonetheless (or, rather, because of this), we need a Deadline-Timeline-Milestones Religion. And our Religion needs a High Priest(ess). She or he schedules people and reviews and report preparation, maintains the timeline, and does a dozen other activities. WITH AN IRON FIST. (The young lawyer-accountant-trainer-consultant who doesn't quickly learn discipline, Marine Corps-style, isn't long for PSF-World ... regardless of his or her IQ and imagination.)

## T.T.D./I-r-o-n Fist!

1. Appoint-Anoint a Scheduling Guru. **ASAP.**

**2. As PSF boss, treat The Schedule and The Scheduling Guru with the utmost visible, public respect.**

3. Make schedules very physically visible. **Consider a War Room.**

4. **Punish** missed deadlines. **Erase** the term "extenuating circumstances" from your group's vocabulary.

5. Reward/celebrate (lavishly!) deadlines that are made. Bigger idea: **Deadlines = Religion.** Punish sins. Reward virtue. Never ignore—or take for granted—either.

6. **ENCOURAGE REALISM!** A big part of making deadlines is not overpromising. Yes, we're in a crunch. Yes, our mission is to routinely do the impossible. But don't let that overanxious, hypertensive youngster sign up for something that she cannot possibly—under any circumstances—do. (This is one more variant of the PSF leader's job as

**Orchestrater of the Rhythm of the WOW! Project Life Cycle.)**

**32a.**

WOW is The Point. But ... big "but" ... it must be Work Worth Paying For.

So ... charge appropriately.
(Aggressively.)
And plan to make a dime ... or three.

### The Nub

I admit it. **I keep score.** Am interested in my speaking fee level ... compared to Henry Kissinger's ... and Colin Powell's. I don't think it's greed. I do think it's an effort to see if I'm still at the top of my game. (Worth the Market Price.)

PSF-ing is Cool. (I hope ... for your sake.)

## And if "it" is Cool ... then Clients should be prepared to ... Pay For Cool.

That is: Pay accordingly for fabulous work.

I.e.: There's a "commercial angle" to "all this." To wit: Charge what you're worth! (For one thing, I need the big bucks to fund the research that leads to more big bucks.)

### T.T.D./ Charge for It!

1. Assess the Market Value for work like yours. **Put in Serious Time on this!**

2. Talk openly to your Clients about fee levels. Don't skirt the issue.

3. **Charge a fair—aggressive—fee for Cool Work!**

# 33.

That sounds rigid. And it is, to a point. Many (*most?*) of the best PSFs—e.g., McKinsey & Co., IDEO, BCG, EDS, CRS Sirrine—have a Characteristic Way of Approaching Problems. Moreover, the likes of McKinsey & Co. lavishly reward those who concoct innovative "frameworks" (a McKinsey term) for effectively attacking classes of problems.

Every project is different. Very true. But one *can* develop tried and (mostly true) ways of looking at categories of projects/problems, of extracting info from clients, of proceeding with research, of framing hypotheses, of presenting conclusions, of engaging clients in the problem-solving and implementation process.

## P.S.: THIS **DOES** APPLY AS MUCH TO THE "HR DEPT." AS TO IDEO OR EDS.

### *The Nub*

When I arrived at McKinsey & Co. in 1974, The Firm was under siege for the first time in decades. The "enemy": the Boston Consulting Group. The problem: BCG had a rigorous "approach" to problem-solving that appeared to be more imaginative than ours.

David Kelley's IDEO Product Development is increasingly being called in to consult Clients on an overall approach to innovation ... **IDEO style.**

In short: There *is* a McKinsey, EDS, Andersen, BCG, Bain, Chiat/Day, CRS Sirrine, IDEO "way of doing things." (Way of approaching problems.) The problems may vary widely and wildly. The approach doesn't. "The Approach" is—literally—worth way more than its weight in purified gold.

## THIS IDEA IS CENTRAL!

Why?

Because in my experience ... **damn few "Depts." have what could be deemed a characteristic, proprietary, valuable "method."**

This is a B-I-G mistake. Unfortunately, one that is not easy to rectify.

Life offers no free lunches. "Approaches" can become rigid, predictable, and stale ... the kiss of death for a PSF. Just as in acting, an overdependence on The Method can rob a performance of spontaneity. In fact, my career at McKinsey & Co. was "made" by attacking "the approach"; such self-cleansing exercises are essential ... and all too uncommon.

Despite the real problems of growing stale, the far bigger issue for most of us (especially budding PSFs) is to develop a **C**haracteristic **W**ay of approaching a problem in the first place!

## THE METHOD

What are typical elements of **The Method?** For starters:

1. **How do we define a problem?** (No small thing!)

2. **How do we state the aims, the goals, the parameters of a particular "case" ... the basis for a project?**

3. **How do we work together with Clients?** (Is there a clear primer for the way Client Involvement will proceed?)

4. **How do we conduct research on the problem?** (How do we insure that we collect knowledge that is, in effect, superior to the collection practices that anyone else uses?)

5. **How do we present our findings?** (At McKinsey there was a clear Presentation Methodology. It was clean, crisp, and ... memorable ... and characteristic of **T**he **F**irm.)

6. **What is the course of a problem-solving exercise?** (How will we work together with you ... over time ... to reach closure on a difficult issue?)

7. **How do we inject originality into the process?** (How do we use outsiders, such as academics,

to bring new perspectives—beyond even our supposedly original perspectives—to the project?)

8. **How do we test our conclusions?** (What is our particular version of the Scientific Method? How do we form hypotheses, test them, be sure of the reliability of our conclusions?)

9. **What is our definition of Quality Control?** (How can you—the Client—be sure that the stuff we are saying is thoroughly and thoughtfully evaluated?)

10. **How do we frame the implementation process?** (What is the extent of our involvement in the implementation process? How do we follow up? Hint: This is where most Professional Service Firms fall down. What do we offer—specifically—that insures that we will *not* fall down in terms of follow-through?)

11. **How do we distinguish our approach from others'?** (The computer company must distinguish its machine from others. And we should distinguish our methodology from others. Do we? Successfully? Clearly?)


## THE MCKINSEY WAY REVEALED! (MOSTLY.)

Not only is there a "McKinsey Way" of approaching problems, but also there is now a book about it! That is, *The McKinsey Way*, by former consultant Ethan Rasiel.

It is not without flaws (e.g., not enough emphasis on implementation and working with Clients), but that's not really the author's point.

"McKinsey is to management what Cartier is to jewels," begins the book's dust jacket squib. There are, indeed, a lot of jewels from The Method in these pages: Aggressive Fact-Gathering. Forces at Work analyses. Initial Hypothesis Generation and challenges thereto. Waterfall Charts. Determining Key Drivers. MECE (mutually exclusive and collectively exhaustive) problem formulation. Just to name a few.

Perhaps you can learn a trick or two from this tome. (It reminded me, for one, of some old—and useful—analytic habits I'd let slip.) More important to my urgings here, you'll get a great snapshot of what a fully developed Methodology can be ... and how it can become the signature of a PSF. (In short: The Methodology makes the man-woman-consultant as much as the man-woman-consultant makes the Methodology. Okay?)

## T.T.D./The Method!

**1. Do you have a codified, characteristic way of approaching problems at "HR Inc."?** Discuss this with your colleagues. (Often there is an implicit methodology—for better or for worse—that needs to be made explicit.)

**2.** Suggested reading: **Donald Schon, *The Reflective Practitioner: How Professionals Think in Action;* Donald Schon, *Educating the Reflective Practitioner.*** These are gems! Make one or both a study group topic. Bigger point: Think *seriously* about this idea. That is, a Proprietary Methodology.

**3.** Invite three or four carefully chosen leaders of local Professional Service Firms for lunch or a half-day seminar. (Pay them if you must!) "Benchmark" their Methodology. And have them critique yours.

## 4. Don't rush. (But don't hesitate.)

Begin a major project to create and codify your Method.

# 34.

Reward marketing excellence.

## PSF-ING HAS A
## CLEAR MARKETING COMPONENT.
## IT IS NOT TO BE DENIED ...
## OR DISMISSED.

PSF marketing ranges from external reputation building (getting quoted in trade journals, producing books, giving seminars) ... to day-to-day Relationship Building while working with Clients on a project ... to networking at conferences, seminars, on airplanes, etc.

### *The Nub*

"Sell" *is* a four-letter word. But not one of *those* four-letter words.

"PSF-ing"**is** selling:

* **Selling** your reputation as Problem Solvers (The Method!, etc.)

* **Selling** your reputation as Revolutionaries

* **Selling** your proven Implementation Skills

* **Selling** your Incredible Talent Pool

* **Selling** your Extraordinary Contacts with Extraordinary People

* **Selling** your Demonstrated Past Successes

PSF-ing is selling: This is one of the tougher hurdles for "conventional" denizens of "Depts." to surmount. That is, realizing that **Sales Is Us**. (It was damn difficult for "official" professional service firms, such as the Big Five accountancies, to deal with this only a few years ago. Now they've become first-class prostitutes!)

It doesn't necessarily mean handing out flyers at the Mall of America. It does mean understanding that you (HR Inc., IS Inc.) have a Genuine Product Worth Paying For to sell.

# It means that "If you build it, they will come" doesn't cut the mustard for your PSF ... any more than it does for Intel or Infiniti.

For the "Dept." turned PSF there's a big element of pride here ... of growing up ... of being unafraid to fully claim your new identity ... and tout your skills ... and shout to the world, "We deliver WOW! big time, and if you want some, h-e-r-e w-e a-r-e!"

For starters, selling means describing our product. Clearly. (What We Do.) Putting together a provocative Sales Kit. Talking sales (future WOW! Projects) with each of our Clients. Going to trade shows and "showing off" our reputation in public ... even if we are still, officially, a "Dept."

## T.T.D./Sell, Baby, Sell!

1. **What is our product?** Start a series of sessions around this topic ... ASAP. (Be specfic. Easier said than done!)

2. **Put together a superb Sales & Marketing Kit. Start now.** (The process of doing so concentrates the mind!) Spend semi-lavishly to make it an unqualified "WOW!" (I.e.: Don't be chintzy!) Consider bringing in an outsider to help you learn the ropes of marketing-selling.

3. As the process above proceeds, talk "sales" with your Clients: Let *them* help *you* define your product and its clear (we hope) advantages.

4. Conduct sales/marketing training sessions. The idea is *not* Arm Twisting 101. The idea *is*: This Is Our Cool Product ... and this is why it's cool/special.

**(Any good career salesperson will tell you that if you don't feel good/great about what you're selling, you'll be a lousy salesperson. It's as true for a professional service as it is for XYZ Widgets.)**

5. Include **"Sales Talk"** (something like this) in your weekly PSF operations-projects review meetings.

# VI. knowledge-
## is-us!

# 35.

It is axiomatic:

### PSF = Intellectual Capital.

Therefore R&D is at the heart of the average professional service firm, or department-turned-PSF.

*Or*: That *ought* to be the case.

Sadly, it rarely is. So, do something about it. Do you—Purchasing Inc. (former Purchasing Dept.)—have a f-o-r-m-a-l research program? *Well funded? Bold?* If not … get cracking.

#### The Nub

Read George Leonard's *Mastery*.

### What "we" do—Purchasing, Finance, IS, Training—is a **C**raft.

(And … yes … capitalize the "C.") A Trade. An exceptional art. As exceptional as throwing or carrying a football. *And* … as exceptional as working in a Pfizer lab.

**I am proud of my Craft.** That is, my ongoing studies of the way organizations work … or don't. I try to learn *something* new … *every* day. (No … damn … joke.) From a hotel experience. Or from reading an academic journal. Or from flying from Albany to Pittsburgh on USAirways.

I am devoted **(yes, "devoted")** to my Craft. As is my wife, Susan Sargent, … a Tapestry Artist. The day you stop growing is the day you start dying. It's a wild, wired, fast-evolving world out there, and what worked yesterday may not today. Anyone who thinks he can rest on his intellectual/social/cultural laurels is not only arrogant but a fool … **and** … mostly … not dedicated to being the **V**ery **B**est **C**raftsperson she (or he) possibly can be.

The overarching idea: **making the idea of Craft-Trade-Mastery central … absolutely central! … to the "Dept."-turned-PSF.**

This is not a "should." This is a "must."

And so … I want to introduce the (big) term … **R&D**/ Research & Development. Say "R&D" and you don't normally think "HR," "Purchasing." Mistake! Big-Damn-Mistake. Okay? If anyone needs to stay on top of R&D-Craft-Mastery it's the Dept.-turned-PSF! You live smack-dab in the White-Hot Center of the Information Revolution. And the White Collar Revolution. Your job can be outsourced … to Indiana or India … in a flash. Ignore R&D-Craft-Mastery, and you may well be obsolete next month (next week? tomorrow?).

I want... every PSFer...

* To be on a path to **Personal Mastery.**

* To be engaged in a **Calling.**

* To be devoted to **Learning New Stuff** ... by hook or by crook ... **Every Day.**

* To **Eschew Complacency** like the plague.

* To take enormous pride in an **Expanding Arsenal of Skills** and knowledge.

* To take the word "<u>R</u>esearch" very seriously ... as seriously as the folks at the Woods Hole Oceanographic Institution. (Why not? *P-L-E-A-S-E.*)

There's a lot of "stuff" to do here. But above all, it's an "attitude thing." An "attitude thing" that says I-AM-A-CONSUMMATE-PROFESSIONAL-DEVOTED-TO-IMPROVING-AND-MASTERING-MY-CRAFT. (As much as the Major League Baseball's "middle reliever" who goes to Spring Training in Florida or Arizona, determined to learn to throw a split-fingered fastball. Surely "your deal" is as cool as his. **No?**)

## T.T.D./ Research-Craft-Mastery

1. Formally assess the Status of Intellectual Capital in your Dept. turned/turning PSF. That is:

Is **EACH** person on a Planned Learning Trajectory Toward Mastery? (Use my term ... "Mastery.") Does *each* person aspire to Towering Competence (an old McKinsey term) at s-o-m-e-t-h-i-n-g?

**2.** Do we talk continually about Mastery … Towering Competence … Personal Distinction … Craft … Curiosity? What they mean?

## Why is the Journey Toward Mastery imperative/integral to Who We Are as Professionals?

Is the specific term "Research & Development" as common as fleas in our Dept.-PSF? Do we talk about what Research & Development means/could mean to us?

# 35a.

## DEVOTE A SIZABLE SHARE OF EFFORT/REVENUES TO KNOWLEDGE DEVELOPMENT.

Professional Service Firm R&D is different. Our folks are spread to the winds, working at Clients' places on projects. Then it's on to the next project without taking a breath. So, how do we learn from one another's experiences?

Answer: It's hardly automatic! *First … we need to take "it"—Knowledge Development—seriously.* Then we need to understand that this goes miles beyond spending megabucks installing the latest, greatest Groupware.

The issue is mostly sociological: E.g., providing strong/unmistakable incentives to those who willingly share what they've learned ... and strong/unmistakable sanctions to those who can't be bothered.

### *The Nub*

You are in Timbuktu.

I am in TimbuckThree. We're both consumed by our WOW! Projects. We're both learning a lot of new stuff. Yet we rarely (*never!*) meet.

## So how do we take advantage—in the best sense—of each other?

This seminal question is bugging firms of all sorts ... especially the Totally Knowledge-Dependent firms.

(I've been worrying about this for close to a decade. You'll find four chapters and 60 pages of *Liberation Management* devoted to "Knowledge Management Structures.")

And my only real answer is: TAKE IT SERIOUSLY. As do Andersen, Buckman Labs (the specialty chemical company), and still far too few others.

My favorite "stories" about Knowledge Management in *Liberation Management* come from old pals at McKinsey and from architects at CRS Sirrine. I find them valuable because they illustrate and emphasize the extraordinary **subtlety** of getting busy people into the sharing/learning mode.

The big idea at McKinsey and CRS Sirrine: **culture!** That is, a Culture that says, in effect: **Share or Die!** Those who take the time from their (ludicrously) busy schedules to share are Heroes. Those who don't are … Goats. Pure **and** simple.

Of course there's lots more to it than that. *Forums* for sharing ideas. (Face-to-face gatherings.) *Formats* for sharing hot ideas. (Electonically abetted.) *Human intervention* to extract good stuff from busy, stressed-out people. ("Flying squads" that visit dispersed folks and shake them down for "lessons learned." The term courtesy Britain's FI Group.) In other words: Knowledge Management permeates every nook and cranny of the organization; "it" is an **(the?)** overriding ethos, permanently on *everyone's* front burner.

The big idea(s):

* We are in the Knowledge Business. **Period.**

* Sharing is *not* automatic. **Period.**

* We need a simple structure and clear incentives to foster sharing. **Period.**

* We need human beings to help *extract* and *package* the "knowledge." **Period.**

## T.T.D./Knowledge Management Excellence!

1. First: Take Knowledge Management seriously. "It" is what we do! *Right?* "It" is a Core Competence. *Right?*

# (Intellectual Capital, the Development and Dispersion Thereof = Us!)

**2.** So: Meet with your colleagues and talk about devices for making sure that we learn from one another, even though all of us are perpetually on the run. Consider software programs such as Lotus Notes.

But, mostly, consider truly "soft" stuff ... incentives that will encourage (and if necessary, force) ludicrously busy people to ... **TAKE THE TIME TO SHARE.**

**3.** There is now a "literature" on Sharing to Create Intellectual Capital. (Start with Thomas A. Stewart's brilliant *Intellectual Capital: The New Wealth of Organizations*.) Study the best practitioners. Apply "lessons learned" from them, even if your Dept./PSF is only a four-person unit.

# 36.

The PSF has something—big!—going for it in R&D. Namely: Projects!

That is: *Every project—no exceptions —can be formulated to have an R&D component ... some intriguing hypothesis to be tested.*

Mostly, it's a matter of developing an instinctive R&D Consciousness. So: What is the R & D component of your current project? Of every project currently in the PSF's Portfolio?

### The Nub

The project involves some changes to a customer service practice. Off to amazon.com. Order a dozen **(!)** books on the topic. One is a real turn-on. Call the University of Michigan prof who coauthored it. Ask if you and two colleagues can visit her in the next two weeks.

Get the whole team tuned into customer service experiences in their own lives ... at dinner out and at the movies this Saturday, at the dry cleaners tomorrow, when that damn automated "service survey" call comes during *Frasier* tonight. Convene a local "mini-summit-conference," one-half day in duration, with top customer service providers giving talks … or, better yet, tours.

Etc.

Etc.

That is: Think "R&D." Constantly. No project is too small to merit serious research. And marvelously wild flights of imagination.

The (big) idea: **Make "R & D chatter" a part of everyday affairs.**

Beyond the individual project is the PSF's Portfolio of Projects. Projects should be selected because of their research potential. Does this project (to create a new training course) give us a unique opportunity to experiment with, say, Web-based, distance-learning course delivery?

## T.T.D./Projects-as-Research-Sites

1. ASAP: **Re-examine e-v-e-r-y ongoing project. Evaluate research opportunities. Redefine ongoing projects (every one?) to enhance research opportunities (e.g.: "Can we work a Web angle into this?").**

**2.** Insist that *every* project team member have an *explicit* "research agenda" for her/his current project. What, specifically, are the Learning and Knowledge Goals?

**3.** Get academic or other "pure" researchers involved in all of your big projects. Consider a Research Advisory Board, which will review all projects and evaluate research potential.

**4.** Work with the Client, starting in the project negotiation phase, to adopt joint research goals for every project.

**5.** In the future, refuse any project with no significant research angle; or recast the project's scope until you can introduce a research angle.

MANTRA: Life is too short to suffer non-learning experiences!

# 37.

*Are "beauty"/"grace"/"elegance" operative words ... relative to every project?*

BEAUTY. GRACE. ELEGANCE.

Not the ordinary staples of Accounting/Purchasing Dept. life. Right? Well ... change that. Design and professional services haven't historically gone hand-in-glove. (Except, of course, for architecture, advertising, graphic and industrial design.) I want you to help me change that. We can't all be great designers. (Understatement.) We can—all!—increase our Design Awareness. We can understand that an unbeautiful project is an abomination. (I'm not kidding about this particular word choice.)

## The Nub

You've run into my buzz saw here. My design + beauty hot button. (Keep those metaphors mixing!)

# I am a design fanatic.

I think "beauty" has a (prominent) place in every project.

E-v-e-r-y.

I think the accountant's work is a work of aesthetics. Accounting: the artful communication of information in a way that assists decision-making. **_RIGHT?_**

Design.

Beauty.

Grace.

Elegance.

_What if…_

You took all these words. Seriously.

_What if…_

Every project … was evaluated on grace + beauty + elegance?

_What if…_

A _designer_ was a formal part of _every_ project team in your PSF?

Design is competitive advantage. Ask Apple. Or Bloomberg. Or Disney. Or Volkswagen. Or Gillette.

Design is a beautiful/functional _billing_ form. Just ask the brilliant professionals at Siegel & Gale. Design is the very essence of a business-process project that matters

... à la the "beautiful processes" that mark Southwest Airlines or Federal Express or USAA.

Design matters as much to service companies (FedEx) as to manufacturers (CAT). It matters (or should!) as much to staff departments/PSFs—which communicate to internal customers via hundreds, thousands of design cues —as to a "line activity" such as marketing.

And yet design typically gets short shrift (especially in "staff" activities). Or worse: Design is used, if at all, as a mop-up tool, to tidy things up after the fact.

**In fact, design's power can only be unleashed when it is a full project partner from Day No. 1.**

# P - L - E - A - S - E.

**T.T.D.**/Design + Beauty

1. NO DAMN JOKE: Evaluate ... formally ... every project in your portfolio on:

* Beauty

* Grace

* Elegance

If "scores" on these dimensions—quantitative!—are low, reframe the project. (As I said: P-L-E-A-S-E.)

**2.** Bring local designers in for lunch or training sessions, to talk about design's possible infusion into project thinking.

**3.** Pick *one* ongoing project as a test case for Design Mindfulness. (Pick a project manager already somewhat predisposed in this direction.)

**4. Put "design" (beauty, grace, elegance, etc.) into every project review meeting.**

**5.** Invite Clients to your design training sessions. Talk with Clients about design implications for their ongoing or future projects.

**6.** Infuse design into your PSF Methodology. (See No. 33 above.) At McKinsey & Co., for example, presentation design was taken v-e-r-y seriously. (When I was on board, the firm had a full-time presentation design guru—Gene Zelazny. And a full-time report-writing stylist guru—Barbara Minto.)

# 38.

Nobody—and no PSF—is "great at everything."

## The essence of PSF market strategy and positioning is "Know thy strengths." (And weaknesses.)

### *The Nub*

David Maister, in *Professional Service Firm Management,* proposes eight possible dimensions of PSF distinction:

* Innovative hiring practices

* Training excellence

* Unique problem-solving methodologies

* Special Client counseling skills

* A particularly robust or valuable knowledge base

* A different approach to project and team organization

* R & D excellence

* Market and/or Client listening skills

Sounds good to me! That is, I can't do any better. The idea: Use this list, or your own variant, to frankly assess your Dept.-PSF's strengths and weaknesses. The main idea here is not filling in holes, but considering where you want to make your PSF mark.

Bigger idea: **"Strategy" is as much the province of an HR Dept. (your HR Dept.) as it is of a division at GE.**

## T.T.D./Strategy and Bases of Advantage

**1.** Using David Maister's list above, begin a careful assessment of your unit's strengths and weaknesses.

**2.** After you have waded through this assessment, launch the critical discussion of "What we want our signature strength to be." Consider seeking advice from Clients and other respected outsiders.

**3.** Does your Dept.-PSF have a formal strategy document, so labeled? And a formal strategy creation and review process? If not … what's the holdup?

**(Note:** "Formal" does not mean hypercomplex! To the contrary … Keep It Simple!)

# VII. talent!

# 39.

Professional Service Firm = Talent. *Period.*

Everybody says, "People are our most important asset." In a professional service firm ... PEOPLE ARE OUR O-N-L-Y ASSET. (Duh!)

My favorite term for all this was swiped from Alan Kay, computer pioneer, who labeled Xerox Palo Alto Research Center founder Bob Taylor a "connoisseur of talent." My take: Accounting Dept. (now PSF/Accounting Inc.) = NBA franchise/ballet company. That is, in basketball and ballet we commonly use the T-word ... Talent. So why not in purchasing departments?

## The Nub

The "PSF business" is the talent business. (Right?) (As in: **What else?**)

The word according to the great adman David Ogilvy (D.O.): "Our business needs a massive transfusion of talent. And talent, I believe, is most likely to be found among nonconformists, dissenters, and rebels."

T.P. (yours truly): SO ... HAVE YOU ADVERTISED FOR/ACTIVELY RECRUITED NONCONFORMISTS, DISSENTERS, AND REBELS (PER SE) ... IN ACCOUNTING ... LATELY?

D.O.: "Hire the kind of people clients don't have and wouldn't dream of hiring."

T.P.: ANY MUSICIANS IN THE ACCOUNTING DEPARTMENT? ARTISTS IN HR? NOVELISTS IN MARKETING?

D.O.: "Tolerate genius."

T.P.: OY VEY ... SO CAN YOU/WILL YOU?

### BECOMING A CONNOISSEUR OF TALENT

If you were a genuine Connoisseur of Talent—like McKinsey & Co. Managing Director Rajat Gupta or Los Angeles Lakers General Manager Jerry West—what would you do?

A Connoisseur of Talent...

1. **Spends lots of time on hiring.** When managers "took on" quality as an/the issue, we learned one thing above all others. It doesn't matter who your guru is —Deming, Juran, Crosby, etc. What matters is your unflinching dedication to the issue. So, too, with talent. The GM of a sports team lives to recruit great talent. So, too, my former colleagues at McKinsey & Co. And ... Gary Withers at Imagination ... and David Kelley at IDEO. Thus: *The* answer for the Finance or HR Dept. head (become/becoming PSF maven!): **T-I-M-E!** In short, a Connoisseur of Talent simply has no higher priority than ... the recruitment and development of ... Talent.

2. **Becomes a student of hiring.** To master neurosurgery, it helps to study the brain. To master talent acquisition and development, it just might help to s-t-u-d-y the field. Right? Yet how many of us can say— with a straight face—that we are true students-of-

hiring? Start with ... Pierre Mornell's *45 Effective Ways for Hiring Smart!* Add Warren Bennis and Patricia Ward Biederman's *Organizing Genius*. And Harold Leavitt and Jean Lipman-Blumen's *Hot Groups*. You wanna master hiring? Study it!

**3. Talks up talent.** Bennis and Biederman say that the leaders of Great Groups "revel in the talent of others." **Love it!** Leaders of great quality programs are broken records ... on the topic of ... Quality. A Connoisseur of Talent is a broken record on the topic of ... Talent.

**4. Thinks like a sports franchise General Manager.** Study the Right Stuff. In this instance ... the naturally talent-obsessed. Benchmark yourself against the General Manager of the Dallas Stars. (Okay? **Why not?**)

**5. Limits the HR role in hiring.** Here's a headline you won't read in the *Miami Herald* anytime soon: HEAT DELEGATE HIRING TO HR DEPARTMENT. A laugh, right? Well, I've told you my bias: There's utterly no difference between you/unit PSF manager and the Miami Heat General Manager. So, forget HR. Hiring is your opportunity. Period.

**6. Writes or reviews all "help wanted" ads herself.** WANNA GET SICK? READ YOUR COMPANY'S "HELP WANTED" ADS! So dry. So dreary. So unimaginative. So ... change all that. Start: today.

**7. Uses plain/sparkling English in want ads and asks for what she wants.** You want "cool people" in finance? Follow the lead of one company and advertise for a "Cool Finance Director." (Why not?) Want a COO with a sunny disposition? Put "sunny disposition" in the ad or write-up for the headhunter.

Bigger message: **Adopt the Plain English Standard.**

Ask for what you want ... in terms a 12-year-old would understand. (Now there's a thought: Have a 12-year-old review all your want ads!)

**8. Develops a Strategic Recruitment Plan.** In Depts. turned PSFs:

## RECRUITMENT = STRATEGY.

So, where is your S-t-r-a-t-e-g-i-c Recruitment Plan for your 14-person IS unit? This is a "strategic issue." Period. Right? (So ... I ask again: Where's the formal plan?)

**9. Recruits from offbeat places.** You want that accounting (training) unit to be wicked cool? So: *Why do you recruit from the same-old-schools?* If you want "stretch folks" in the Dept./PSF, then you're gonna have to look in s-t-r-e-t-c-h places.

**10. Becomes de facto CDO (Chief Diversity Officer).** Creativity—in any endeavor—grows out of the combustion created by strange mixes. It is that simple. So: If creativity and innovation are your gig ... then Diversity must be your middle name. Young ... and old. Women ... and men. All colors, backgrounds, ethnicities. **RAINBOW CITY!** Political correctness? Not for me! Creativity and innovation are my shtick. So Diversity is necessarily my passion. (Make it yours.)

**11. Thinks and recruits MI/Multiple Intelligences.**
Harvard professor of education Howard Gardner says
there are at least seven varieties of intelligence.(Logical-
mathematical, linguistic, musical, spatial-artistic, bodily-
kinesthetic, interpersonal/others, intrapersonal/self.)
Problem: We typically emphasize but one ... logical-
mathematical ... and thereby denigrate most of human
capacity in the process. Study Gardner. Act accordingly.
Hire diverse intelligences.

**12. Thinks arts. (Damn it.)** My mantra:
Every Accounting Dept./PSF needs a musician! (See
above.) I admit that I've become obsessed with this issue.
We have so much to learn—in Accounting or HR or IS—
from the arts. To get yourself thinking about this important issue, read David Gelernter's *Machine Beauty*. Bottom line: Connoisseurs of Talent are connoisseurs of
those with backgrounds/foregrounds in the arts. Okay?
(If not ... why not? Think about it. Discuss it. Join me:
Obsess on it.)

**13. Gets the best folks involved in recruit-
ing, hiring, and talent development and men-
toring up to their eyeballs.** In short: MAKE
TALENT EVERYBODY'S BUSINESS. Recruiting—and development—should be in everybody's "job description."
And that includes the newest hire. No kidding.(No kidding
= **Measure it. From Day No. 1.**)

**14. Turns the pay scale upside down.** In pro
sports, the coach-manager is paid but a fraction of his
stars' salaries. So ... why not HR? Why not ... Purchasing?
Message: REWARD TALENT. And not just in the NBA. The
"great" trainer ... purchasing officer ... finance guy/gal is

worth her/his weight in gold. And then some. Pony up. Managing is important stuff. "Talent" is arguably more important. Thence: Pay accordingly.

Author Hesh Kestin, in *Twenty-First-Century Management,* on Computer Associates: "If this sounds like professional sports, the analogy is apt. The [star] engineer's value to CA is as high as that of a star quarterback to a pro football team, and both in pro ball and at CA, stars are sought out, developed, and compensated accordingly."

**15. Launches and nurtures a "Great Place to Work" PR campaign, including institutional advertising.** Sell the fact that you are a Cool Place for Cool People. Sell it shamelessly. If you *are* cool, spending lots of energy making it known is as invaluable an activity as branding. In fact, in the new brain-based economy cool-place-to-work is at the heart of branding! (In PSF-land: Cool Place for Cool People = The Brand.)

**16. Works on R.I.P.s (Renewal Investment Plans) with all employees.** Talent—in the NBA or on the stage or screen—either gets better or gets out. That's not been the case, except marginally, in the HR/Finance world. No more! The message to one and all must be: You will renew yourself—big time!—or be sidelined as quickly as an out-of-shape pro athlete. The secret? The usual: attention. In this case, attention to renewal per se. My favored device: a formal **R**enewal **I**nvestment **P**lan ... taken very seriously ... and made a centerpiece of formal evaluations. (No renewal "success," no stay. Gotcha!) (See also our *the Brand You50* ... for a real diatribe on this subject.)

**17. Uses Project selection and staffing as a key development tool.** You = Your portfolio of projects. Thus: Talent Development = Project selection. The Connoisseur of Talent uses the employee's prospective projects as the basis for carefully developing that individual. Thus, project assignments are partially (mostly?) based on development goals.

**18. Evaluates all managers on their talent development skills.** If Connoisseurship of Talent is the mark of the effective PSF, then the *top* trait of *every* manager is her/his *demonstrated* talent recruitment and development skills. These skills should be used as the premier basis for managerial selection and subsequent evaluation. (Once again, conjure up the pro sports team's General Manager as exemplar.)

**19. Rewrites values-vision document to reflect "talent obsession."** "People are our most important asset." Read this boilerplate so much I'll toss if I see it again. On the other hand ... the Talent-Based Enterprise (a.k.a. PSF) needs to put ... um ... Talent at the tiptop of its Corporate Consciousness. By definition. So Talent must top the values-vision statement. (Then ... obviously ... put your money/time where your collective mouths are.)

**20. Micromanages all promotion decisions with an eye on talent recruitment and development skills ("Nancy demonstrates a passion for talent development" ... or she doesn't).** I am a fanatic about delegation/decentralization. This, however, is *the* exception to my rule. We need—must have!—Connoisseurs of Talent in *all* managerial roles.

Thence we who lead must insure that *all* promotions go to ... Connoisseurs of Talent. (Simple, eh?) The way to do that: Micromanage the promotion process. Promotions decisions come only once in a blue moon. I.e.: Don't waste a single one!

**21. Makes recruitment and talent development a staple of every operating review.** This is a variant of ... SPEND TIME. That is, put recruitment and development on every agenda. Daily. Weekly. Monthly. Once you start talking about "it" ... obsessively ... you'll start doing something about "it." Which is the whole point!

The above list is not perfect. Nor is it meant to be. It aims to prove that I can shout, "CONNOISSEUR OF TALENT," and then suggest a *practical* action plan to back up my rantings. Thence my goal here is modest: to get your mind geared up around this vital **(!)** topic.

## T.T.D./Connoisseur of Talent

1. Read the above. Carefully. Is that you? If not ... why not?

2. Get the whole gang together. (Connoisseurship of Talent is a Team Sport.) Review the entire list above.

**Score your group—quantitatively—on each item.** Pick two or three items of particular importance. Set a 30-day deadline to put together a game plan to improve unit/PSF performance on these priority Connoisseur of Talent dimensions.

# 39a.

Or: IT'S THE PEOPLE, STUPID.

### The Nub

We're *all* in the professional services. That's the reason for this book…and the message of the (humungous) White Collar Work Revolution of the early 21st century. Therefore: We are all in the Talent Business…as much as Hollywood or Broadway or pro sports.

Thence any (PSF) winner will become a Magnet for Talent. It's the big sister, I suppose, of No. 39 above. It is the ultimate goal statement:

## WE WANT TO BE A PLACE WHERE COOL PEOPLE WANT TO BE.

(Or some such.) The starting point: boldly stating this —in strong language like that above—as an explicit aspiration.

There's an enormous amount of hard work to be done. It takes far more than a proclamation, to be sure. But an uncompromising determination to be a Very Cool Place to Work is a good place to start.

What are the characteristics of a joint that becomes a Magnet for Talent? It's a place with ...

* A portfolio of **S**eriously **R**ockin' **P**rojects.

* Good Vibes ... a sense of urgency, high energy, flexibility, friendliness.

* Diversity on the brain: on the lookout for renegades and backgrounds of the most fascinating sort.

* A youthful attitude. Age ain't bad. (I ain't young.) But ... high energy and youthfulness do go hand-in-glove. (And, often, the evidence says, only youth has the naïveté and nerve to undertake the "stupid" causes ... that will change the world.)

* A commitment to a Quest. A stated determination to Be the Best/Coolest.

* Room to learn new, cool stuff.

* A high-tech-as-all-get-out vision.

* An opportunity to Own a Piece of the Rock.

## T.T.D./ Magnet for Talent!

1. The PSF's management team must lay out a vision that is inspiring. A talent-centric vision.

## (COOL DUDES/DUDETTES DOIN' COOL STUFF.)

And ... immediately ... take some "first steps" to demonstrate that a bright new day is dawning. (Formally declaring yourself a full-fledged PSF might be a good starting point, not so incidentally!)

**2.** Weed out dead/dreary wood: projects, clients, staffers. High morale is magnetic … and nothing kills it faster than Merchants of Malaise. Remove "sad dogs who spread gloom," counsels advertising legend David Ogilvy. (As, for what it's worth, do I.)

**3.** Make the n-e-x-t hire count! **Now** is the time to prove you've changed. Leave a slot or slots unfilled—and take the heat from your stressed-out co-workers—until you find someone who symbolizes exactly what you want the place to "feel like." PLEASE DON'T COMPROMISE ON THIS. THE MOMENT IS NOW. (*Hint:* Pitch in yourself to help those who are left short-staffed while you search for just the right rockin' soul.)

**4.** Form a **Y**outh **C**ommission of three or four **H**ot **Y**oung **T**urks to lead the hiring effort. And make their projects examples of the bold, state-of-the-art work we intend to perform. (State-of-the-art work = Essence of talent magnetism.)

**5.** Notice that I haven't stressed pay and perks. It's not that they are unimportant. Not at all. It *is* that they don't come first. Heating up the Work Itself is the starting point. Period. It's the nub of becoming a Magnet for Talent.

# 40.

IDEO Chief David Kelley takes the ideas above a step farther.

It's not enough to hire a cool mix of cool people.

You've got to keep mixing them up ... to keep them and their projects fresh/surprising. Kelley practices Talent Connoisseurship as well as any NBA General Manager. Then he juxtaposes the talents in all sorts of crazy-quilt ways to provide fresh perspectives on every project.

## *The Nub*

## Think weird!

Remember David Ogilvy: Hire the kind of people clients wouldn't have the nerve to hire.

Creativity—by definition—comes from mixing things up. Constantly. Creativity comes from naïveté ... looking at tired, old issues afresh.

The IDEO story, alluded to above, is one of the best. So, too, Britain's Imagination. And the world of Apple's Steve Jobs. IDEO's Kelley, Imagination's Gary Withers, and

Apple's Jobs are Masters of Mix. Wizards of Weird. Nabobs of Naïveté. All three are explicitly determined to:

* Hire a combustible mix of backgrounds.

* Stir and spice the mix constantly.

* Bring fresh (naïve) perspectives to any and every problem.

This is not a side game for these three. It is an Unabashed Core Competence.

My advice: Follow their lead. **Copy them.** Shamelessly.

## T.T.D./Master of Mix!

1. Make weird mixes the heart of your "talent strategy." Start now. (If there are no openings, bring in weird outside advisers. See No. 27 above.)

2. Begin with an assessment of the backgrounds of your current team members. You'll doubtless be surprised at some offbeat skills that have been hidden from view. (*Idea:* Exploit them!)

3. Examine each project line-up carefully.

## Can you deftly introduce some talent-from-left-field?

This can be tricky, because current staffers may feel slighted or threatened. So keep folks informed and try to get them to become co-initiators of the new addition(s).

Begin by asking whom they would pick if they could have some additional resources. (Don't precipitously plop some "fabulous new talent" down in their midst; you're sure to encounter major resistance that may well negate any gains the talent provides.) Work with clients to get them similarly to add fresh talent at their end of your joint teams.

# 40a.

No turnover (or low turnover), no automatic refreshment.

### The Nub

Can you imagine a pro baseball (basketball, etc.) team —or theater company—with no or low turnover? Of course not. Right?! Or a pro team or theater company not taking a chance on a couple of stellar rookies? (Of course not. Right?!)

Such completely talent-dependent enterprises, often with market values in the hundreds of millions of dollars, live (or die) based on the boldness of roster improvement and talent-mix adjustments.

Likewise, it's no accident that almost all law firms— and many other professional service outfits—live by

(1) "up or out" and (2) top-dollar-for-top-rookies. These totally talent-dependent organizations also depend (totally) on big-time "roster" renewal. And (obviously): Stasis is death!

# Welcome to Talent World!
# Welcome to Professional Service Firm World!
# Churn (of the roster sort) = Renewal.
# Stasis = Death.
# (Quickly.)

## T.T.D./ Roster Churn!

1. **Squarely face the facts above.** What holds for the Los Angeles Lakers and Detroit Lions holds for "Purchasing Inc." So: How do we deal with it? Foster it? Make it happen?

2. Bosses: Begin to instill, via the performance evaluation process, some version of "up or out." (There's really no choice.) See, perhaps, our companion *the Brand You50*; we argue that it is in the self-interest of every "employee" to think/act like a growth-obsessed, independent contractor.

3. Discuss all this—via an "all hands" Brown Bag Lunch Series—with partners in local law firms, the General Manager of the local pro team, a theater director.

# 41.

(Or be in the process of becoming so known.)

## Every individual **MUST BE** committed to a radical program of growth.

Everyone must think Me Inc./Brand You. I.e., have the mindset of an independent contractor. Think … fresh … fresh … refresh … refresh: "We" (PSFers) are in the Intellectual Capital Business. Period. We had therefore damn well better be out front.

That is:

**(1)** Everyone must have "a rep" … stand out as the "Coolest Person in New England on executive compensation issues" … or some such.

**(2)** Every one of our professionals is, therefore, a brand ("Brand You" is my favored term) in her/his own right … or in the process of becoming one.

**(3)** He/she/everyone should therefore think of themselves as independent contractors/CEOs of Me Inc. … who just happen to be hanging out at HR Inc. at this moment.

**(4)** All this necessarily puts the pressure on each of us to make a radical commitment to renewal ... by everyone. THIS ALL ADDS UP TO A PASSION FOR—AND AN OBSESSION WITH—PERPETUAL PERSONAL AND PROFESSIONAL GROWTH AND RENEWAL.

### The Nub

I want to make the language as strong as possible here.

MANTRA: **WE INSIST THAT EVERYONE AIM TO BE FEROCIOUSLY GOOD ... AT SOMETHING.**

McKinsey & Co. called it "towering competence." I don't care what you pick:

* Ferociously good

* Towering competence

* Mastery

* Seriously-good-at-something

* Super hot shit

* The best

The White Collar Revolution will wipe out indistinct "workers." And reward the daylights out of those with True Distinction.

So: **Choose sides.**

As PSF chief, it's the ultimate no-brainer: We cannot afford anyone on the payroll who doesn't aim for … clear distinction.

This is not a new idea among … **chefs … professors … actresses … tenors … surgeons … linebackers … gardeners … house painters.** It seems as though it is a more or less novel notion, however, among HR, IS, and Purchasing "staffers" who labor in "Depts."

To put it mildly, our nemesis Dilbert doesn't honor **G**reat **C**raft. Well, things have got to change. Fast. Which is, if you've got the nerve, very cool. And very liberating.

**It is the sound of freedom: free to be special and feisty and obsessed with being the best, not a yes-saying cipher-bureaucrat doing mediocre work.**

Death (professional) to the Organization Man! Babbittry Be Damned!

Whoa, what a screed. But I do mean it. The essence of PSF-ing is folks who are—each and every one—determined to be of surpassing value.

### T.T.D./The Relentless Pursuit of Surpassing Value!

**1.** Toss out … now! … your current personnel evaluation scheme. Start building a new one that rests on the

**Relentless Pursuit of Surpassing Value.**
(Think about using those precise words.)

**2.** Okay, okay: So you won't merrily scrap the current evaluation system (No. 1 above). Well, at least **begin** the dialogue with every individual in the "Dept." about Rabidly Pursuing True Distinction. Make such "conversation" part of daily chatter.

**3.** Play with terms: Ferociously Good. Towering Competence. Mastery. Pursuit of True Distinction. Rabid Pursuit of True Distinction. Relentless Pursuit of Surpassing Value. Talk about what each could mean. Individually. For the group.

**4.** Work the Relentless Pursuit of Surpassing Value into: (1) explicit goals for (2) every member of (3) every project team. **Start ASAP.**

**(5.** Tom's self-serving suggestion: Buy each staffer a copy of the companion to this book, *the Brand You50*.)

**6.** Have everyone develop a **Bold Personal Mission Statement.** Take this very seriously: For God's sake … don't let it become bureaucratic! Suggested reading: Stephen Covey's *The 7 Habits of Highly Effective People*. Get folks thinking/talking about their passions outside of work. The idea here: to translate that ardor/obsession/commitment to their professional quests to be the best.

# 41a.

### The Nub

Jean Lipman-Blumen and Hal Leavitt have given us a marvelous book: *Hot Groups.* One of the most interesting points they make: Admiration beats affection.

That is, Hot Groups—and Hot Professional Service Firms—are task-obsessed. Project maniacs. Rabid for Results. Members deeply admire Unstinting Contributions by their fellow team members. But that doesn't necessarily mean they want to go on a Caribbean cruise with them.

Great PSFs are built on respect and admiration for the talent, passion, commitment, and energy of one's co-workers. And if affection develops along the way ... fine and dandy. But if not ... fine, too.

I'm certainly not saying that "chemistry" is unimportant. I *am* saying that the important chemistry is the Chemistry of Commitment and Accomplishment.

Some championship professional sports teams are "love-ins." (Or so I've heard.) But the ones I've known up-fairly-close are "respect-ins." There's a difference that gets to the heart of a Great PSF: WE ARE HERE—PRIMARILY—TO WORK OUR BUNS OFF TO PRODUCE SERIOUSLY GOOD/COOL/MEMORABLE WORK. THAT WE CAN BE COLLECTIVELY PROUD OF FIVE YEARS FROM NOW. If we all become best friends in the process, great! But that is *not* the name of the game. In fact, mature team players/WOW!-creators quickly learn to overlook the annoying traits and habits of their fellows—as long as said fellows are delivering cool/memorable work.

## T.T.D./A Performance Ethic

**1.** PSF Boss: Sit with your colleagues and launch The Great Dialogue. (Never-ending.) What would it mean/feel like if this place were the Accounting Dept. equivalent of a Super Bowl team? What would it mean for interpersonal relationships? Where is the line between admiration and affection?

**2.** Talk about Great Groups (Cub Scouts or Brownies, theater groups, etc.) you have each been part of. What makes for a Great Group? (Commitment to Great Accomplishments is at the top, I bet.) Translate these lessons into your budding PSF and current projects.

**3.** As usual: Talk about this with *every* Client. After all, our project work is joint ventures. (Right?) So how do we *jointly* turn each project into a Great Group?...aiming at a Great Accomplishment?

# 42.

## CHAMPION PASSION.
## CHAMPION PERFECTION.

We want—nay, demand—passion and a willingness to live on the edge. We also want—nay, demand—exceptionally "professional" behavior. So? That's PSF life! Amazing freedom to do Cool Stuff. And equally amazing demands that we do it ... Obsessively Well.

### The Nub

I am a pro football fan. And I've especially admired Bill Walsh's San Francisco 49ers and Tom Landry's Dallas Cowboys. Both coaches were imaginative as Hell. (Walsh re-invented offense. Landry re-invented defense.) Both teams had passionate field leaders: Montana (Joe) of the 49ers, Staubach (Roger) of the Cowboys. And both "pioneering" coaches were also no-baloney, hard-assed, detail-obsessed perfectionists of the first order.

My top bosses at McKinsey & Co. were *wildly* intellectual. *And* ... insanely demanding.

I've got a pal who writes and reviews books (she's won awards for her criticism). Her pet peeve about way too much of the stuff she reads (fiction and non-fiction): "The corners aren't mitered." What she means is that the author didn't sweat the details ... didn't tie up the loose plot ends ... left in sloppy sentences ... and "small" research errors. Right on! And how depressing! It's the kind of work we all see too much of these days ... and it makes me go ballistic ... and it has no place in *your* PSF (that is if you aim to survive the White Collar Revolution).

It is **the** great paradox: Living on the edge. A rebellious streak a mile wide. And a mile deep. *And* insane self—and group—pressure to insure the corners are mitered.

## T.T.D./Living the Passion/Perfection Paradox

1. The Big Idea: Yank this paradox w-a-y out of the closet. Talk about passion/imagination. Talk about performance/perfection. Talk up "outrageous" standards ... on *both* dimensions! Make the conversation an active part of every-day-in-PSF.

2. Put *every* piece of work your Dept.-turned/turning-into-a-PSF does to the "Are the Corners Mitered?" Test. That means a final, detail-obsessed review to make sure that *every* comma is in place, *every* loose end tied up, *every* question/problem (and *every* potential question/problem) addressed and answered.

3. **And** ... put e-v-e-r-y project through the WOW/Beauty/Does It Matter? Test.

4. Use both Tests religiously.

# (Mitered Corners.)
# (Does It Matter?)

## 43.

### CREATE STORIES/MYTHOLOGY AROUND "PROJECT WINNERS."

Create stories about and a mythology around those who have done great things ... in service to their Clients ... in Pursuit of WOW! You're creating a Rockin' PSF:

# All special-cool places need a Mythology.

(You can't fake this. God help you if you try to. But if you're straight ... it's a powerful spur to creating a powerful culture. Hey, we all need heroes.)

### *The Nub*

We're deeply into Cool? *Right?* PSF = Cool.(Former) Accounting Department = Cool Professional Service Firm. *Right?*

"Cool" places live on "cool" sagas. Legends. Tales of derring-do. All-nighters. Incredible screwups. Last-minute death (professional)-defying heroics.

I don't want to romanticize this too much, but My McKinsey ... San Francisco Office '74–'81 ... was a romantic place. My first boss, Jim Crownover, said, "We're the movie stars of the business world." Typically cynical girls and boys at business schools swooned at the mention of the name McKinsey. (And "swooned" isn't too strong a word.) And that is P-R-E-C-I-S-E-L-Y what I want your new-born Dept.-turned-PSF to become. (And what I believe it **can** become.)

The PSF bedrock = Projects.

# The mythologic bedrock: stories about Cool-WOW! People at work on Cool-WOW! Projects.

Every great organization needs myths, legends, heroes. So … talk about it. **Work on it.** Consciously.

## T.T.D./Stories to Live By

1. No. **You can't fake it.** And if you try, you'll negate the whole point by destroying your credibility. (See above.) But "it" *is* powerful. So think about "it." Be on the lookout for "it." Take advantage of "it" when "it" happens. **"It"?** Cool stories about Cool people doing Cool work on Cool projects.

2. Launch an informal newsletter. Or weekly e-mail. ("The Cool Stuff Review.") (Hey, it's a big deal: How many accounting "departments" do you know of that have newsletters?) Get in the habit of sharing cool stories. I.e.: Build the mythology! Have an Annual Awards Banquet! (Sales "Departments" do. Why not HR? Why not Finance? **Damn it!)** Honor heroes. I.e. redux: Build the mythology!

# 44.

Train in ... Project Creation ... and ... the Methodology of Problem Solving. Train in ... Implementation. Train in ... Client Relations and Client Development. Train in ... Project Management ... and ... Project Membership.

## THE POINT: THIS "STUFF"—THE STUFF OF PROFESSIONAL SERVICE FIRMS—IS TRAINABLE!

First, you've got to believe that "it" *is* trainable. (I'm amazed at how few firms have solid project management training ... or *any* project management training, other than how to use scheduling software.) Once you pass the "can be done" hurdle, the next step is a long-term commitment to developing a *full* curriculum covering the sorts of topics enumerated above. Then ... find the time to deliver the training!

### The Nub

Arthur Andersen, EDS, and Computer Associates are among the (few) PSFs famous for their training programs. **A.K.A.: Boot camps!**

All three firms have a Point of View...a Methodology. And they Teach the Hell Out of It. In my experience, this is rare (understatement!) in the average "Purchasing Dept."

My goal: **a complete rethinking of Professional Service Training. I.e., training for the (new) white collar worker.** (New)(Mostly) topics for the curriculum include:

* WOW Projects
* Project Creation
* Project Execution
* "Selling" a WOW Project
* Mission, Value, and Point of View in a Professional Service Firm
* Building Hot Groups
* Collaborating with Clients
* Methodology: Approaching a Project
* Project Research
* Developing Hot Talent on the Fly
* Working with Cool Outsiders

So, are *these* topics staples of your training agenda in the Purchasing "Dept."? If not...am I all wet? **(Or are you?)**

## T.T.D./Total Training Overhaul!

1. Look at my list above. Improve on it! Add topics that are specific/unique to your PSF! Seriously consider **...stopping all training** ... until you can concoct an imaginative agenda.

2. Study Andersen/EDS/Computer Associates and the like. Benchmark against training at top professional service firms.

3. IS YOUR *EXPLICIT* TRAINING GOAL TO CREATE A SUPERCOOL/SUPERINVENTIVE PSF ... WITH INCREDIBLE TALENT ... TAKING CLIENTS TO PLACES THEY'D NEVER DARED TO DREAM OF? (If not ... why not?)

# 45.

## It can be done.

Despite the big vote for formal training above, on-the-job training remains the No. 1 crucible for would-be PSF WOW!-ers. And at the top professional service firms, OJT is Goal No. 1: *Get even the most unseasoned professionals into a project management "job" quickly.*

If you are determined, you *can* quickly get *every* team member into a genuine leadership/ownership role relative to *some* project sub-sub-task.

Bottom line: *Nothing builds skills and confidence as surely and quickly as responsibility for delivering results in the real world!*

### *The Nub*

In their wholly original *Corporate Strategy and the Search for Ethics,* Ed Freeman and Daniel Gilbert write about

## <u>P</u>ersonal <u>P</u>rojects
## <u>E</u>nterprise <u>S</u>trategy:

*Corporations are human institutions.... Our view of the corporation is fairly simple. It is a means to facilitate the realization of the projects of certain persons called "corporate members." A corporation is simply one way that we achieve our projects. Stated somewhat differently, persons are only passing through corporations on the way to their respective ends.... Corporations can be thought of as sets of agreements among the members to achieve their projects.*

That is:

# The "cool organization" is a place where individuals come—for a while—to Express Themselves and to Grow ... via Projects that Matter.

Or, per me: Welcome to Professional Service Firm world ... at its (occasional) best.

More fuel for the fire. Careers guru Tim Hall says:

—*"Firms will provide opportunities and resources ... to enable the employee to develop identity and adaptivity and thus be in charge of his or her own career."*
—*"If the old contract was with the organization, in the protean career the contract is with the self."*

Add it up and you have what I call: PROFESSIONAL SERVICE FIRM AS "OPPORTUNITIES STRUCTURE."

At McKinsey & Co., the powers-that-be used to laugh (or sigh), especially in the big offices like New York, about the "baronies," the practically autonomous "mini-firms" that surrounded a powerful partner. Law firms are (exactly) the same.

And it's not all bad. In fact, it is (mostly) good. That is, professional services are less "professional" than "personal." (Whoops, I've just let loose The Dirty *Big* Secret.) That is, "associates"—the typical professional service firm term for entry-level employees—gravitate to Cool Seniors who become their mentors. Why? Because they're attracted to the excitement ... the power ... and the chance to learn/grow/stretch via real-world challenges.

Professional Service Firms are not structureless. To the contrary! The system of ranks may be fairly vague ... but the Pecking Order is not. At their best, real Professional Service Firms are, above all, Meritocracies. They have (very) low tolerance for non-performers, age 23 or age 63.

Is this "good" or "bad"? Both. Doubtless. It puts crushing pressure to perform on one and (mostly) all. **The bad news:** Stress City! **The (very) good news:** Performance-Growth-Meritocracy City. (Whiners and politicians have a relatively tough time in the project/performance/Client-centric environment of a decent Professional Service Firm. Hooray!)

## RANKS AT MCKINSEY & CO.: A CASE IN POINT

The rank structure at McKinsey is not brilliant. It is simply typical of a Professional Service Firm. There are four main levels:

* **Associate.** This is the entry-level job, the cannon fodder on the project team. One arrives as an Associate ... and stays that way for a year or two.

* **EM/Engagement Manager.** This is the "team leader"/"project manager." After putting in a couple of years in the trenches, one takes charge of a modest-sized project ... or, remember, Engagement (in McKinsey-speak). This is a job one performs for the next three or four years.

* **Principal.** Getting "elected" (the exact right word! It's sort of papal. In fact, v-e-r-y papal) to "partner" is the big deal in any professional service firm. McKinsey is relatively standard in having two levels of partner. "Junior" partners are officially "Principals." This means super-Project Manager, with responsibility for client relationships.

* **Director.** This is the Senior Partner. The Director-Rainmaker has responsibility for several, often sizable Clients. The line between Principal and Director is not clear ... in any way that can be logically explained. Principals who do "damn good stuff" and lasso (and retain) serious Clients become ... Directors.

As I said, there is nothing "brilliant" about the structure. But it **is** an opportunity structure that centers on the Big Two of PSFs: Projects and Clients. The progression: Team Member, Team (Project) Leader, Client Relationship Executive, Rainmaker. As usual, it's a rank structure that is at (extreme) variance with that of a typical "Dept."

## T.T.D./Performance-Opportunity "Culture"

1. Is your unit/department/now PSF an "opportunity structure" ... per the ideas above? Are staffers lining up/signing up for Cool (the coolest) Projects? Do they have a meritocratic/growth-through-increasingly-cool-projects mentality?

2. Do you (PSF Boss) talk up meritocracy/progress-through-cool-project-performance at every occasion? (If so ... is your talk *credible*?)

3. Is the "rank structure" perfectly attuned to Progressing-Through-Projects-of-Increasing-Importance? And Client-Development-Activities-of-Increasing-Importance?

# 46.

It's not just the loud ones—the great presenters—who are honored.

## If Clients-R-Us . . . then Listening-Had-Damn-Well-Better-Be-Us. I.e.: Love the quiet ones . . . with Big Ears.

In professional service firms it's always tempting to heap the praise on that masterful presenter . . . who effortlessly awes the Client. (And they are great to have on your team.)

On the other hand, that discerning Client is mostly awed because of the extraordinary insight the project team exhibits.

And such insight is often due—in my experience—to the quiet team member, with those Big Ears, who listens to the Subtle Vibes so brilliantly, who unearths the curious character in the bowels of the Client organization who knows all the secrets and gives him/her an extensive/empathetic hearing.

Message: HONOR THOSE B-I-G EARS!

### *The Nub*

I admit it. I like the flashy-bright people. The ones who star at repartee. Who wear their (formidable) intelligences on their sleeves.

But: I am also *reformed*.

I *have* learned my lesson.

Over *and* over.

There's this guy/gal on the team. Mr./Ms. Antiflash. Quiet as the proverbial church mouse. To him/her, "repartee" is a four-letter word.

And yet again...*and again*...he/she comes up with exceptional insights. It finally dawned on me, about year 15 into my professional service career: **T-H-E-Y HAVE B-I-G EARS.** (And relatively small egos.)

Delivery of professional services is about True Partnership in Problem Solving with the Client. Partnerships are always two-way streets paved with bricks labeled

communication/

## communication/

### communication.

That is:

## Excellence = Excellence-in-Listening.

Ah, yes, it's the quiet one! Who leaves the two-hour interview, having failed to publicly exhibit her surpassing intelligence. But who has truly Tuned Into the Client and his ambiance. Who has read between the lines. Who has walked away with incredible, counterintuitive insights. God love her. (And God damn the ones—like me!—who can't keep their mouths shut. And who often end up expending considerable effort extracting their shoewear from their XXL mouths.)

## T.T.D./Listeners-from-Heaven!

1. First, take my line of argument seriously. Trust me:

**There are planet-class Listeners. _And_ they are rarely flashy. _And_ they are worth their weight in gold (x10).**

So look for 'em. (Listen for 'em?) They are your lifeblood!

2. Publicly, as PSF boss, praise-the-blooming-daylights out of the Quiet Listener ... who provides the exceptional insights.

3. More generally:

# Train in listening skills. It is possible!

(That is, even the noisiest of us can get a little better ... if we are conscious of the problem and the magnitude of the opportunity.)

# 47.

The quiet ones—those listeners—often are on the short end of the Honors List. So, too, the geeky types. Just plain antisocial. Wouldn't (*couldn't!*) schmooze a Client if their lives depended on it. Day-after-day-after-day they pound away at the keyboard... and unearth the most amazing, pertinent information imaginable ... time-and-time-and-time-again.

Message: HONOR (HEAP ADORATION UPON THE SHOULDERS OF) THOSE HOPELESSLY ANTISOCIAL GEEKS!

## *The Nub*

In my McKinsey & Co. days ... and to this day ... I suppose I am numbered among the flashier types. (At least among the l-o-u-d-e-r ones.) And often "we" become leaders. And often we hire in our own image. And often we make a **b-i-g** mistake!

The PSF needs its Front Women, its Rainmakers. But it equally needs its Total Weirdos ... who ask the tough (non-P.C.) questions ... and see the world through a different lens.(Maybe we are finally learning this...as geek-ish Bill Gates's net worth soars to $100 *billion*.)

My point: We need the real freaks...if we are going to come up with truly freaky-new solutions to problems.

Find 'em.

Love 'em.

## Pay 'em.

# Promote 'em.

T.T.D./Blessed are the Talented Geeks-Freaks!

1. Does your Dept./PSF have its full share of Misfits? The strange ones, who are a little embarrassing around "the suits," but who are responsible for 85 percent of your gang's truly profound insights?

2. **Are you looking ... actively ... for such effective misfit-geeks?** In (very) odd corners?

3. Are geeks/freaks obviously welcome in "your place"? What have you done (specifically—don't B.S. me on this) to make your place comfortable for them?

# 48.

Demand … the impossible.

From everyone. (Obviously: starting with yourself.) "I make myself a relentless architect of the possibilities of human beings."—Benjamin Zander, Conductor, Boston Philharmonic, a Professional Service Firm.

BE GREAT! (Why not?)

EVERYBODY! (Why not?)

It's not heartless and it's not about lip service. It's a true commitment to excellence.

And why the Hell not?! Hire great folks! Offer great training! Surface great clients! Invent great projects!

And then … kindly request growth + excellence.

Okay?

### *The Nub*

We want cool!

We l-o-v-e cool!

We expect cool!

We **demand** cool!

This is *our* (PSF) house ... and we want it to be ... g-r-e-a-t. Right?

T.T.D./Cool!

# Make it clear:
# This is/will be a remarkable place.
# And we ... desperately want
# y-o-u to be a b-i-g and
# responsible part of it.

# VIII. it's ours!

# 49.

## The Nub

* WOW!
* Beauty
* Impact
* Distinction

## T.T.D./ WOW!

So ... measure ... each + every activity/project against:

* WOW!
* Beauty
* Impact
* Distinction

Do so ... **formally ... quantitatively ... regularly.**

# 50.

The mantra-to-end-all-mantras in PSF-land:

"We *are* HR **Inc.**

"This is *our* joint.

"It is *our* life.

"*We* are in charge.

"Excellence is in *our* hands ... to choose ... or lose."

## *The Nub*

# *It's ours.*

**T.T.D.**/It's Ours!

It's *ours*. So ... live accordingly.

### ADDRESS TO SENIOR PARTNERS
### OF A MAJOR INTERNATIONAL
### PROFESSIONAL SERVICE FIRM

In early October 1998 I spoke for an hour to the 275 senior partners of one of the world's most prestigious professional service firms. This was the challenge I laid down ...

* Are you up to the biggest-deal-since-the-cavemen-began-bartering? (The word according to Sandia National Labs' chief economist Arnold Baker.) Are you part of the revolution … or merely a "competent spectator"?

* Are you "too big to be cool"? (Tom note: The firm employs thousands.)

* Are you wrestling with the eternal struggle: Caution in pursuit of "brand protection" versus stepping out toward fundamental innovation?

* Are you aware of the perils of success? The word according to Gordon MacKenzie, former Hallmark creative guru (from his book *Orbiting the Giant Hairball: A Corporate Fool's Guide to Surviving with Grace*):

—Passion begets success

—Success begets success formula

—Success formula begets isolation from passion, vision, and innovation

—Isolation begets atrophy, decay, a fading away.

* Are you creating WOW! I know that you are doing "excellent" work … but are you doing **great** work? I.e.: **Work that is … Awesome … Amazing … Stunning?** (Hey … these *are* stunning times.)

* Are you hiring a combustible mix of talents? "Tolerate genius."—David Ogilvy. So … do you? "Expose yourself to the best things humans have done and then try to bring those things into what you are doing."—Steve

Jobs, on hiring artists, musicians, etc. for his (computer/software) product development teams. How many artists have you hired lately?

* Are you a talent magnet? Do the very "coolest," not just the "best and brightest," want to work for you?

* Are you taking real risks? If you are not provocative, you are—de facto—dead. If you are not pissing (lots of) people off, you are not making a difference.

* Have you fired any big clients lately? (An imperative, per David Ogilvy, when you become co-opted and/or Clients start to wear you out.)

* Are you holding yourself to the highest imaginable standard? This means regularly asking: WAS IT—Project/Projects—WORTH DOING? (Henry James's ultimate challenge to artists ... beyond "Was it good work?")

* WILL THE PROJECTS THAT YOUR ASSOCI-ATES ARE WORKING ON ... RIGHT NOW ... BE REMEMBERED WITH PRIDE TEN YEARS FROM NOW? (T-H-I-N-K A-B-O-U-T I-T. AND DON'T MESS WITH ME!)

* Are you thinking epitaph? (You ain't that young.) "He had a $10 million net worth due to 'diligent work.'" TP: Yuck! (I.e.:

### But Did It ... Make a Difference?)

**"Something great"**—Hiroshi Yamauchi, the Nintendo chief, to a leading game designer (on what he should create next)

**"Immortal"**—David Ogilvy, on what kind of ad he wanted his head creative guy to make for children's clothing made from Viyella

**"Amaze me"**—Sergei Diaghilev, the great ballet director's challenge to one of his dancers

**"If you ask me what I have come to do in this world, I who am an artist, I will reply, I am here to live my life out loud."**—Émile Zola

## Nirvana (per this book):

* **WOW!** people
* Performing **WOW!**/Beautiful Projects
* With **WOW!** impact
* For **WOW!**-able clients
* …and **Redefining** what
* organizations **Are**
* And **How** they do business.

I know *you* can do it.

# The Movement**!**

How audacious! Start a Movement?! We plan to do just that.

Title: # The Work Matters**!**

Or: The Anti-Dilbert Movement.

We are sick and tired of whining about lousy bosses. (Or companies.) It is—as we see it—our life. To live ... or lose. To form ... or allow to be formed.

Dilbert is hilarious. (I.e., on the money.) And there's the rub. Dilbert stands not only for cynicism (an emotion I appreciate) but for the de facto acceptance of power-less-ness. And that is where I draw the line!

## It is my life**!** To live ... fully. Or not. And I damn well intend to live it fully. And I don't think I'm alone.

So ... my colleagues and I are ... audaciously ... start-ing **The Work Matters!** Movement. And we invite you to join us. Cost of membership: **the time it takes to type www.tompeters.com onto your computer.** So ... welcome aboard! (P.S.: You may have noted the oversized **!** in the paragraphs above. No accident. That is our symbol ... the exclamation point ... about as far from Dilbertville as one can get, eh?)

There's not much published on professional service firms. And that's an understatement! Nonetheless, what follows should prove to be of value if the PSF bee gets into your bonnet:

**TRUE PROFESSIONALISM,** by David Maister (New York: The Free Press, 1997). **MAISTER IS PSF-MAN!** And this is his best and most thoughtful work.

**MANAGING THE PROFESSIONAL SERVICE FIRM,** by David Maister (Boston: Maister & Associates). A superb collection of Maister's best articles. All good stuff!

**OGILVY ON ADVERTISING,** by David Ogilvy (New York: Crown, 1983). David Ogilvy at his best on a number of topics, not least: how to run an ad agency.

**THE McKINSEY WAY,** by Ethan M. Rasiel (New York: McGraw-Hill, 1999). This book does *not* reveal McKinsey's secrets; nonetheless, it does a good job of explaining McKinsey's approach to problems (which no one has heretofore even attempted to do). McKinsey presentation maestro Gene Zelazny's **SAY IT WITH CHARTS** (Homewood, IL: Dow Jones-Irwin, 1985) is a good companion to Rasiel's book; as is **THE MINTO PYRAMID PRINCIPLE** (Southport, UK: Financial Times Management, 1995), from McKinsey writing guru Barbara Minto.

**EDUCATING THE REFLECTIVE PRACTITIONER,** by Donald A. Schon (San Francisco: Jossey-Bass, 1987). A masterpiece, which explores the training of professionals. (Also see Schon's **THE REFLECTIVE PRACTITIONER** (New York: Basic Books, 1983).

**HOT GROUPS,** by Jean Lipman-Blumen and Harold J. Leavitt (New York: Oxford University Press, 1999). PSF per se is not the topic here; but the Hot Group idea, masterfully presented in this book, fits my scheme of things to a tee.

**RAIN MAKING: THE PROFESSIONAL'S GUIDE TO ATTRACTING NEW CLIENTS,** by Ford Harding (Holbrook, MA: Adams Media, 1994). This is an unabashed "sales book"... a true rarity in PSF-land. A worthy read.

**FINDING THE WINNING EDGE,** by Bill Walsh (Champaign, IL: Sports Publishing, 1998). Hall of Fame San Francisco 49ers coach Walsh ("the genius") commanded one of the world's most effective "PSFs." This detailed description of the NFL coach's approach to everything has many lessons for all of us in PSF-world.

For sources cited, see **www.tompeters.com**

# ACKNOWLEDGMENTS

Erik Hansen...project manager for this book and chief architect, along with Julie Anixter and Ken Silvia, of **The Movement!** (I.e.: The Work Matters!)

Sonny Mehta..."the publisher"...who's always up for something new and interesting. Edward Kastenmeier (Knopf) and Sebastian Stuart (himself!) ... for inspired and meticulous editing. (Sebastian often out-me's me!)

Esther Newberg at ICM, who pushed this book project/ series with her usual flair and tenacity. Knopf Design Guru Chip Kidd ... who invented the look and feel of this series. Pat Johnson ... believer and Knopf marketing maestrina. Larry Holman and Bunny Holman at WYNCOM, for providing the Lessons in Leadership seminar series... the perfect platform for presenting these ideas to frustrated corporate staffers.

Thanks to Patrik Jonsson and Jim Napolitano from Mulberry Studio for translating my original hen scratchings—yes, all of my first drafts are Bic on Yellow Pad— into a usable ms. Thanks also to Elyse Friedman, Vincent Renstrom, and Martha Lawler for editorial expertise. Thanks to Sue Bencuya ... for fact-checking ... Katherine Hourigan, without whose assistance none of this would actually have happened ... Mel Rosenthal, who helped eliminate errors and inconsistencies ... Andy Hughes and Quinn O'Neill, who turned these words into the bound book you now hold in your hands ... Merri Ann Morrell, whose herculean efforts helped make these books possible. And Ian Thomson and Michelle Rotzin … for minding the store at The Tom Peters Company in Palo Alto.

And: Katz (Jon Katzenbach), Bob Waterman, Allen Puckett, Allan Kennedy, John Stewart, Jim Balloun, Jim Crownover, and Jim Bennett, who taught me "PSF-ing" at McKinsey & Co. And Marvin Bower … who created modern McKinsey and, thence, the modern PSF; Marvin's presence has been transmitted to many, many pages of this book.

**And:** Susan Sargent, best friend and litmus test … with regard to damn near everything.

Tom Peters,
West Tinmouth, Vermont,
30 July 1999

Tom Peters is the co-author of *In Search of Excellence* (with Robert H. Waterman, Jr.) and *A Passion for Excellence* (with Nancy Austin), and the author of *Thriving on Chaos*, *Liberation Management*, *The Tom Peters Seminar*, *The Pursuit of Wow!*, *The Circle of Innovation*, and the *Reinventing Work* series. He is the founder of the Tom Peters Company, with offices in Palo Alto, Boston, Chicago, Cincinnati, and London. He and his family live on a farm in Vermont and an island off the Massachusetts coast, thanks to the information technology revolution. He can be reached at **tom@tompeters.com.**

# tompeters.com

And now it's easy to get WOW!ed with Tom anywhere:

<u>See</u> Tom Peters at a live one-day seminar near you!
www.lessonsinleadership.com
1-800-873-3451

<u>Bring WOW! Projects to your desktop computer</u>!
www.ninthhouse.com
1-800-304-4951

<u>See</u> Tom on Yahoo! Broadcast Services this fall!
www.leadership.broadcast.com

<u>Schedule</u> Tom to talk to your group!
michellerotzin@tompeters.com

<u>Learn about Training and Consulting</u> for your business!
www.tompeters.com
1-888-221-8685